withdrawn

PRACTICAL
MINDFULNESS

PRACTICAL
MINDFULNESS

withdrawn

Consultant: **Ken A. Verni, PsyD**

Penguin
Random
House

DK LONDON

Senior Art Editor Anne Fisher
Managing Editor Dawn Henderson
Managing Art Editor Christine Keilty
US Editor Rebecca Warren
Jacket Art Editor Harriet Yeomans
Senior Producer Stephanie McConnell
Senior Producer, Pre-Production Tony Phipps

Publisher Peggy Vance
Art Director Maxine Pedliham
Publishing Director Marie-Clare Jerram

Produced for DK by

COBALT ID
Art Editors Paul Reid and Rebecca Johns
Editor Marek Walisiewicz

Illustrator Trina Dalziel

Writer Mike Annesley
Consultant Dr. Ken A. Verni

First American Edition, 2015
Published in the United States by DK Publishing
345 Hudson Street, New York, New York 10014

DK books are available at special discounts when purchased
in bulk for sales promotions, premiums, fund-raising, or
educational use. For details, contact: DK Publishing Special
Markets, 345 Hudson Street, New York, New York 10014
SpecialSales@dk.com

Printed and bound in China

All images © Dorling Kindersley Limited
For further information see: www.dkimages.com

A WORLD OF IDEAS:
SEE ALL THERE IS TO KNOW
www.dk.com

CONTENTS

DISCOVERING MINDFULNESS

TOWARD A MINDFUL YOU

MINDFULNESS MEDITATION

MINDFULNESS LIFE SKILLS

MINDFULNESS WHEN YOU NEED IT

FOREWORD

Mindfulness can be described in many ways. It is a practice of purposefully paying attention in the present moment and bringing a nonjudgemental, compassionate awareness to the nature of things. It is a way of being, a way of relating to our inner and outer experiences, and a coming to our senses, literally and figuratively. At the same time, it is nothing at all, nothing but a rediscovery or a remembering of our natural, inborn capacity to be fully awake in our lives, in contact with things in a direct way without the filters of concepts, past experiences, or likes and dislikes.

This way of seeing is immediately available to all of us at any moment. Try it now if you like. After reading this paragraph, let your eyes move away from the page and let your gaze land on something nearby. Offer it bare attention, seeing it as if for the first time, leaving labels and associations aside. Softly notice its shape, color,

texture, and the space it occupies. Practicing further, you might also notice thoughts crossing your mind, your attention wandering to something else, or feelings arising in response to your sensory contact with the object. Simply come home again and again to a direct experience of the object you have chosen. Give it a try now, then return and reread the instructions above before trying again. You can use the same object or a different one each time.

What you just engaged in was a mindfulness practice. You picked an "object of attention" to help anchor your awareness in present moment experience and you observed what happened in your mind, body, and heart. Most likely, much of what you observed reflects some of the elements of your everyday experience, such as distraction, desire, aversion, restlessness, doubt, or boredom. Yet there may have also been

moments of just seeing. This is what is meant by mindfulness "practice." It is called a practice because when we do it in a consistent fashion, we get multiple opportunities to practice with "the stuff of life." Over time we can gently shift our relationship to this "stuff" and learn in a safe, gradual, self-paced way how to respond—instead of react—to the habits and "frequent flyers" of the mind. We learn to cultivate choice and develop a greater sense of efficacy and balance in our lives.

In this way, we gradually restore a healthy, friendly relationship with ourselves, begin to feel less alienated and isolated (from ourselves and others), and reconnect to our own deep intuitive wisdom and creativity. This practice is an inner journey, and perhaps the most important journey of our lives—a thought elegantly captured by the American monk and writer Thomas Merton: "Of what use is it that we can travel to the Moon, if we can't cross the abyss that separates us from ourselves?".

This book can serve as a thoughtful guide and introduction to the journey of cultivating greater mindful awareness in your life. In clear language,

it describes the essence and the practice of mindfulness and suggests action plans for building it into your life. But like any journey, it is important that you follow your own wisdom as well and pay particular attention to what feels helpful and what does not.

It is also important to attend to the way that the judging nature of the mind can subtly turn your mindfulness practice into just one more "self-improvement" project. Mindfulness offers much more: it is a way of simply coming to know yourself and things just as they are, moment by moment, and opening to the wisdom that naturally arises when one cultivates a compassionate curiosity toward the human experience.

One final description of mindfulness may be useful here. Above all, it is a path of the heart—a practice of loving awareness—that offers to hold any and all experience in a compassionate, spacious embrace. So let the heart guide you through the practices and reflections offered in this book and in each of your moments. Beginning here... now.

Ken A. Verni

DISCOVERING MINDFULNESS

MINDFULNESS IS A UNIVERSAL,
MODERN WAY TO ENHANCE
LIFE. ITS PRACTICE CAN MAKE US
CALMER AND MORE CENTERED, AND
IMPROVE OUR PHYSICAL WELL-BEING.

A BEGINNER'S GUIDE TO THE HERE AND NOW

HOW MINDFULNESS CAN ENRICH YOUR LIFE

The mindful way to well-being is life-changing. If you choose it, you'll need to follow a routine of short mindfulness meditations. Alongside that, you'll need to become aware of any ingrained habits of mind that have stopped you, so far, from living life to the full.

The idea of mindfulness is very simple: you pay close attention to an experience in the present moment, while allowing yourself to be open-hearted and "spacious." This last word needs a little explanation. Our pure state of mind is spacious, but over time, as we accumulate life experiences, certain habits of thinking form and solidify. Mindfulness meditation, practiced over a period of at least a few weeks, can break down these inner structures and return us to our original openness. That's why mindfulness practice has been proven effective as an antidote to all kinds of negative

> Mindfulness changes your sense of who you are in relation to your own life and to other people.

TRUTHS AND MYTHS ABOUT MINDFULNESS

Mindfulness is a modern practice that involves paying full attention to your experiences, both good and bad—it's not a state of mystical bliss or spiritual transcendence. It has no religious dimension.

MINDFULNESS IS
- Recognizing feelings without becoming caught up in them
- Identifying yourself as who you truly are—and not identifying yourself with your feelings or mistakes
- Living more in the moment and less in the past and future
- A way to cultivate happiness that's suitable for all.

MINDFULNESS IS NOT
- Emptying the mind or stopping thinking
- A relaxation technique, though it will make you more relaxed as a by-product
- An escape from personality— it *reveals* to us our personality
- A charter for living life without planning—you can plan in a mindful way, just as you can learn mindfully from the past.

mindsets, including poor self-esteem, high anxiety, low levels of vitality and engagement, and mild to moderate depression.

Mindfulness changes your sense of who you are in relation to your own life and to other people. It also gives you better access to your full potential,

YOUR FIRST MINDFUL MOMENTS: AN INTRODUCTION TO PRACTICE

"Practice" is an essential word in mindfulness, and in any form of meditation or mental training. It implies repetition (as well as a way of being), and that's apt, since you can only change your mindset by doing an exercise regularly, perhaps daily. However, this initial practice, below, has a more limited aim: it is a basic introduction to what mindfulness involves. If any thoughts or emotions come into your mind while doing it, be aware of them but don't dwell on them: return to your focus and let them pass away.

1 Sit down at a table with a small object in front of you—a cup, mug, or glass, or a salt or pepper shaker will do.

2 Look closely at the object for a few minutes, taking in everything about it you can see—without touching it or moving it. Just think of what it looks like without judging its beauty or utility.

3 Focus on your sensations. Remaining still, close your eyes and be aware of any physical sensations—the places where your body touches your clothes, and where you feel pressure from the chair or floor.

4 Spend a few minutes focusing your mind on what you can hear—it might just be the sounds of your breathing, or it might be your neighbor's radio or the whine of a plane.

5 Look back on what you've just experienced. By focusing on an object, on sensations, and then on sounds, you've given yourself a break from your preoccupations. Over time this can be a major source of mental refreshment.

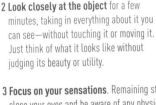

particularly in terms of relationships and personal goals. To live more mindfully is to live more richly, with more skill, ease, and flexibility. You gain in self-understanding, and can use that as the foundation-stone for a happier life. When challenges occur or you encounter threats in life, you'll be less likely to find them overwhelming; and when opportunities arise, you'll be able to recognize them and welcome them joyfully into your life. Habits of mind will remain but exert less of a tug, giving you freedom to cultivate healthier ways of thinking.

Introducing the present

The main ingredient in the mindfulness recipe is the present moment. It isn't that you need to concentrate on the moment itself, since a moment is impossible to pin down. Instead, what you do is focus on your experience in the present, forgetting about past and future, or time itself passing—as well as about any thoughts or emotions that enter your mind. You might be focusing on something you're doing, or looking at, or listening to, or feeling as a sensation, such as your breath: you're being mindful if you concentrate on this with relaxed but purposeful attention. Formal mindfulness practices, including the ones in this book, take the body, the acts of breathing or walking, or objects as favored points of focus.

NEW MOMENT, NEW YOU

THE BENEFITS OF MINDFULNESS

Thinking skills

Better memory

Quicker reaction times

Better mental stamina

Enhanced intuition

Quicker mental processing

Enhanced brain function

Better concentration

Better decision-making

Listing the benefits of mindfulness feels a lot like quantifying the value of love: its worth is intrinsic to itself, so trying to tease it into separate strands is missing the point. However, mindfulness has been much researched, and a checklist of its proven benefits is useful as a motivating call to give it a try.

The pioneer of modern mindfulness, Jon Kabat-Zinn, wrote candidly that you don't have to like mindfulness practice, you just have to do it. He knew that some people found mindfulness a chore, but he was also very aware of its tangible benefits.

His early work is now supported by numerous scientific studies that show that mindfulness practice enhances mental and physical well-being. Research highlights its success in reducing stress and anxiety, attributing this to a reduction in levels of cortisol—sometimes called the "stress hormone"—in the body. And since stress tends to undermine the effectiveness of the body's natural immune system, mindfulness can also be linked with improved immunity.

The health benefits of mindfulness are undeniable, and range from stress and pain relief and improved sleep patterns to a greater likelihood of breaking out of depression or addiction. Beyond the province of health, though, is the vast realm of well-being, where the advantages of mindfulness practice multiply dizzyingly. In making us more attentive, more grounded, more self-aware, more confident, more decisive, and less bound to the habits of the mind's autopilot, mindfulness opens up for us a new way of living. We learn to deal more effectively with life's pitfalls and setbacks, but also to derive more satisfaction and enjoyment from life's pleasures. No longer held back by negative patterns of thought about ourselves, we set ourselves on the path to releasing our full potential.

> "Mindfulness refers to keeping one's consciousness alive to the present reality. It is the miracle by which we master and restore ourselves."
>
> Thich Nhat Hanh

Health and well-being

Reduced levels of anxiety

Resilience to fatigue

Reduced stress

Relief from depression

Reduced levels of pain

Better control over addictions or
self-destructive behavior

Stronger immune system

Improved heart and circulatory health

Better sleep

HOW MINDFULNESS MINIMIZES PAIN

Some of the health benefits of mindfulness result from the way in which it trains us to be less reactive—for example, to our emotions. Pain, like an emotion, tends to draw us into itself to do battle with it. In seeking to block out a pain, we might clench our muscles in that part of the body; or we might engage in combat with the pain, sometimes angrily. These reactions drain us of energy without relieving the discomfort. The mindful way is to accept the pain and separate out the emotional reaction it causes. No longer reinforced by emotion, the pain becomes weaker.

CIRCLES OF WELL-BEING

The benefits of mindfulness radiate out from being healthier, calmer, and fitter (if keeping fit is where we choose to concentrate attention) to having a set of highly effective lifestyle skills that make every aspect of our everyday lives more rewarding.

Self-awareness and life skills

Better self-knowledge

Freedom from habitual responses

Better mastery of emotions

Better communication

More effective public speaking

Better listening skills

Increased empathy

Better self-reliance

More emotional intelligence

Increased resilience in adversity

Happiness and fulfillment

Higher self-esteem

More self-confidence

Increased enjoyment of leisure pursuits

Better relationships

More satisfaction from work

Better focus on goals

Release of full potential

MIND FULL OF THOUGHTS

ATTENTION AND DISTRACTION

Mindfulness is about directing our attention inward, in the present moment, and making discoveries about what sensations we're feeling, and what thoughts and emotions we're having. When distractions occur—a bird singing, a memory surfacing—we just let them go.

The mind is an instrument, but also an inner landscape, which thoughts cross like tumbleweed. However intently we try to concentrate our minds on a task, some thoughts will come straying into our inner field of view from time to time, distracting us from our focus. We have a choice: we can react to them, or we can take a more mindful route—we can simply notice them, without judgement, staying in the present moment as we do so.

Our thoughts and our direct experiences, though separate, are engaged in a perpetual interaction. While the human mind seems to be the ultimate multitasker, it can in fact only hold one thought at a time. It gives the impression of multitasking by performing the most incredible juggling act: from one moment to the next, some thoughts rise while others fall, to resurface later. But within this confusion, certain traceable lines of thought, or sequences of sensation and thought, will be operating, and these often originate in direct experience. This may seem a strange concept, which can be best explained through an example.

Radio, potatoes, wood, supper

At home, peeling potatoes while listening to the radio, we might hear unexpected noises from our backyard, cutting through the newsreader's voice. Within a moment or two we recognize the loud percussive chucks of our partner chopping wood. And that takes our mind off the news and makes us call that person to mind, and perhaps wonder whether the barbecue grill has already been lit. We're thinking thoughts about thoughts, and though the newsreader continues reading the bulletin, we're no longer taking any notice of it. We may have momentarily stopped peeling potatoes, since we're

We can react to thoughts; or alternatively—and this is what we do in our mindfulness practice—we can simply notice them, without judgement.

absorbed in wondering if we'll be eating late this evening. What has happened here is that our attention is no longer in the present—it has wandered into thinking about the future. Through mindfulness, we can control our attention in such situations: we can choose to go out to talk to our partner, or we give our attention to the radio, or focus on peeling. We can opt to exclude the wood-chopping from our minds (we may not even notice the sounds after a couple of minutes) and put off the question about supper until later.

Choosing your focus

In mindfulness practice you choose where to place your focus. You direct your attention there, but you don't worry if distracting thoughts or feelings, or perhaps unexpected sensations (like a clock chiming or phone ringing), cross your inner landscape. You note such unbidden experiences but exercise your choice not to engage with them. Instead, you redirect your attention to the matter at hand—your chosen focus—whether it's your breath, body sensation, or something else entirely.

RIPPLES OF THOUGHT

The way our minds process sensations, thoughts, and emotions can be compared to a raindrop falling onto a pond. Direct experience—our sensations or emotions—are where the droplet hits the pond. The inner circle of ripples represent our initial thoughts, while the outer circles are the thoughts that develop from there. Thoughts tend to carry on generating further thoughts, unless we direct our attention somewhere else. Mindfulness practice gives us the means to do this in our everyday lives.

MINDFUL DROPS
The calm surface of water disturbed by a falling droplet of experience has become a common symbol of mindfulness.

DIRECT EXPERIENCE
BODY SENSATIONS   EMOTIONS

SIMPLE THOUGHTS
RECOGNIZING   CATEGORIZING

THOUGHTS ABOUT THOUGHTS
INTERPRETING   CONNECTING   REMEMBERING   IMAGINING   PROJECTING

SILENT WITNESS
FOCUS WITHOUT JUDGEMENT

Mindfulness involves paying attention with a focused mind, in the present moment, without judgement. But what does this really mean? And why should the question of judgement arise when we're focusing, say, on our breath or our body sensations?

Imagine that you're meditating mindfully, concentrating your attention on your breath as it enters and leaves your body. Sitting down, you now direct your thoughts to the pressure of the edge of the chair against your lower thigh. That pressure is there every time you sit on the chair to eat your dinner or write a letter, but you usually don't even notice it, or attend to it at all. Bringing such sensations into the spotlight of consciousness—and keeping them there—is an example of paying attention with a focused mind in the present moment.

Wandering thoughts and feelings

Very few of us are able to completely control our thinking. Put simply, our minds tend to wander. So as you sit, mindfully focusing on the sensations in your thigh, you're likely to experience distractions. Some will be prompted by external events, such as the chiming of a distant clock or the sound of the postman opening your gate; others will come out of your preoccupations.

STOPPING SHORT OF JUDGEMENT

What does non-judgement look like in practice? Consider this imaginary scenario: your wayward brother is coming to visit this weekend. You know you must speak to him to help him move his behavior onto a more even course. Before he arrives, you engage in mindfulness meditation, but your focus is trespassed upon by thoughts; these trigger emotions that in turn lead to reactions—judgements. In mindfulness practice you would simply acknowledge the thoughts and emotions: you would not react or get tangled up with judgement.

THOUGHT	EMOTION	JUDGEMENT
"I wonder how I'll start the conversation."	Anxiety about a difficult task.	Deciding to limit the conversation.
"He's making it hard even to arrange the conversation."	Impatience.	Deciding to put off another arrangement.
"What is he likely to say?"	Trepidation.	Deciding I mustn't let it get to me.
"Last time we spoke, I wasn't honest."	Annoyance with myself for not saying what I meant.	Thinking that I mustn't be so hard on myself.
"He's having a very difficult time right now."	Concern for brother's well-being.	Wondering if he needs counseling.

JUDGEMENT TRASH CAN

In your mindfulness practice, sensations—part of your present experience—will inevitably rise up into your awareness. It's good to acknowledge these visitors (highlighted in bold in the thoughtstream below). Resist the temptation to get drawn into making judgements about them (in gray type). These will disrupt your meditation and lead you to other unwanted thoughts.

There's a smell of flowers. I must have left the living room window open.

There's an ache in my neck and shoulders— I'd better go for a massage.

There's a green glass vase on the table. It looks expensive.

That was the cat meowing. I wonder if anyone's fed her.

Fragments of thought or emotion will emerge unbidden from the kaleidoscope of your unconscious. Often, they will be trivial—thoughts about where you left the scissors, or what time you need to pick up your daughter from her class; sometimes they will be vague anxieties that you can't quite pin down; and at other times they will be more troubling emotions, such as anger or fear. Sometimes thoughts will visit alone, but often they'll be accompanied by emotions. If you say to yourself, "I really don't want this thought or emotion in my head now, it's spoiling my first mindfulness practice," you're making a judgement—an unspoken comment. In mindfulness, you're not supposed to make such judgements on intruding thoughts or feelings, so what should you do with them? The answer is that you register your awareness of them, and notice exactly how you experience them, but you consciously refocus your awareness on your physical sensations—your breathing or the sensation in your thigh. You don't engage with the thoughts or feelings, but let them fade away. This is mindfulness in action.

HALF TIME
Research indicates that our minds are unfocused for about half of our waking hours.

THE POWER OF AUTOPILOT

PATTERNS OF THOUGHT, FEELING, AND BEHAVIOR

Autopilot is the opposite of mindfulness: it's a state of mind disengaged from the present and stuck in habits formed long ago. Letting go of our automatic behavior enables us to escape the pull of the past, and offers us a better chance of happiness.

Autopilot enables us to carry out basic functions in life—dressing, walking, climbing stairs—without taking up all our attention. It helps us to learn complex new skills, such as driving a car or touch-typing. Once we apply ourselves to learning, the skill starts to become automatic—for example, you drive to a destination remembering almost nothing about your journey. This is often desirable because it frees the mind to move on to other things that require conscious attention. However, autopilot can also work against us, particularly in the ways we process our emotional lives. We often reflect on how we felt, or feel, about past experiences, and try to apply our conclusions to attain happier outcomes in the future. The problem occurs when we repeat this process automatically, offering the same emotional reactions to similar situations, even though the outcome last time was far from ideal.

Dissolving negative patterns

When on autopilot, the mind steals its reactions from the past. We don't realize, when we are in auto mode, that we have a wide range of options

FIVE SMALL WAYS TO TURN OFF AUTO

Dissolving the habitual responses of your emotional life through mindfulness will take a great deal of practice, but, for the moment, here are five ways to refresh your everyday routines:

1 LEAVE YOUR MOBILE PHONE AT HOME

This may feel unsettling, since we're all used to the sense of constant connection. Carrying our mobile devices, we're never truly solitary. Rediscover what it feels like.

2 TALK TO A STRANGER

Spend a few minutes having a chat with someone you meet while shopping or traveling to work. Autopilot can undermine our sense of connection, except to friends, family, and work colleagues. It's good to realize that others may have something to offer.

available. The truth is, there's no need to be hurt by a situation just because it's hurt us before.

Consciously setting out to break established patterns by taking determined action is not necessarily the best way to overcome them; paradoxically, the patterns may be strengthened by such active resistance. What's needed is a new, more mindful, way of thinking. By training ourselves to live in the present moment, and relate to our experience with acceptance rather than judgement, we become more grounded and more nimble in our responses. Autopilot dissolves when mindfulness takes over at the wheel.

> The mind on autopilot steals its reactions from the past. We don't realize, in auto mode, that we have a wide range of options available.

AUTO VS. ENGAGED: CONTRASTING STYLES

If we live our inner lives on autopilot, we end up repeating our mistakes, experiencing the same crises over and over, and failing to move on. Mindfulness brings our pattern of emotions into awareness, equipping us better to realize our potential.

THE AUTOPILOT WAY	THE MINDFUL WAY
We react with habit.	We respond with awareness.
We emptily relive the past.	We fully live the present.
We neglect realities.	We accept realities.
We miss the details.	We notice the details.
We re-enact established patterns.	We see the big picture.
We have limited choices.	We have many choices.
We repeat past emotions.	We have fresh emotions.
We neglect our potential.	We realize our potential.
We enjoy life's pleasures less.	We enjoy life's pleasures more.

3
DO SOMETHING NEW WITH YOUR PARTNER
Take your loved one to a kind of event you've never tried together before—anything from a hiking trip to a football game. Relationships can get stuck in routines. A novelty like this can jolt you out of your habits and reawaken your bond.

4
BREAK A REGULAR JOURNEY
Stop en route and explore a new area before continuing. Start out earlier if necessary. Walk around observantly. Try to find something you can take from the experience: perhaps a store you might visit again or the color scheme of a house.

5
DO THAT BIG CHORE
It's autopilot that makes us procrastinate, avoiding uncomfortable experiences for as long as possible. Since it has to be done, schedule a time as soon as possible. Don't let it hang over you threateningly. Do it with your full attention.

Mindfulness means purposefully paying attention, in the present moment, without making any kind of judgement.

A THOUSAND LEAVES

FINDING THE MOMENT IN REPETITIVE CHORES

Any repetitive chore—from painting a wall to doing the dishes—offers a chance for mindfulness. Leaf sweeping has Zen overtones: clearing leaves from ornamental patterns raked in sand was essential in a Japanese temple garden. Try it as an introduction to mindfulness in action.

British crime writer Agatha Christie famously said that the best time to plan a book is while you're washing the dishes. It's easy to see where she was coming from. The word "mindless" readily attaches itself to everyday chores, so if you can disengage from a boring and repetitive task and do it perfectly well on autopilot, then why not? You'll get the dishes clean at the same time as sorting out problems that require your conscious attention.

Why then, would you wish to make a mindless task mindful? It's bad enough sweeping the yard without having to inhabit every moment of the chore as if it were precious. The moments would be precious, you might say, if you didn't have to spend them brushing leaves away, and trying to enjoy it.

Over and over

This parody of a popular, uninformed view is worth taking seriously for the questions it raises. Would you really miss a valuable experience if you did some thinking while sweeping the leaves? Wouldn't you get the boring task done better and more quickly by tackling it head on, without mindfulness? And once you've swept a thousand leaves, would sweeping another few hundred really make the experience any richer?

Anyone who's experienced the value of mindfulness should be able to tackle these questions without difficulty, since their intuition will be attuned to how it operates. First, they'll know that mindfulness is not prescriptive. If someone has a menu to devise in their heads or a speech to plan, there's no reason at all why they shouldn't work on this while leaf-sweeping—especially if they've found they can think more

Mindfully sweeping leaves isn't just about getting to know what they really look like or subjecting yourself to a session of mental austerity—your mind is sure to wander and you can learn a lot from its unauthorized detours.

effectively in such circumstances. Any feeling of guilt about this choice would be unnecessary. Mindfulness does not impose choices upon you in the way that your nagging, logical mind may do.

Thought and distraction

There's a big difference, however, between consciously using the sweeping time for thought and going out there with no intention other than to get the job done. People doing a routine activity often drift into thoughts of planning, and find themselves repeating the same thoughts unhelpfully—until thinking becomes as automated as sweeping. Also, their mind is likely to stray into pointless worrying. In any case, if you take your mind off a repetitive job, you're likely to do it more slowly and less efficiently.

Nobody is going to concentrate 100 percent on leaf-sweeping, but if you do opt to sweep in the moment, with purposeful attention, and without judgement (not thinking "This is so boring" or "I wish I could be curled up by the fire"), you will create a stable place for your thoughts to settle. If they wander, and you start worrying about something, the mindful way is to observe those worries without getting drawn into them, and then gently, if you choose to, bring your focus back to your brushing. By the end of the session, you'll have enjoyed a different kind of double benefit—getting the job done and spending some healing time (it is healing, though you won't know this yet) in the now.

Bringing mindfulness to a routine task gives you the opportunity to be present in the moment, in a way that, over time,

will help to rebalance your mind, bringing the benefits described on pages 18–19 of this book. Mindfulness in the long term will perform a gradual makeover on your brain.

GARDEN MEDITATION
Thoughts and emotions will enter your mind as you sweep. Choose to observe them, without letting them take over, before returning to your sweeping.

LIVING THE DREAM
MINDFULNESS AND HAPPINESS

Happiness was once thought to be a personality trait; you might have a happy, sunny disposition or a sad, dark one. However, recent studies by behavioral psychologists show that it is far from a fixed trait and that it can be closely linked with mindfulness.

It is a common saying that money can't buy you happiness. You could say the same about pleasure, too. Many people whose primary goals are wealth, physical thrills, or sensual excitement, eventually become jaded and listless. When you're on the hedonistic treadmill, what you think will make you happy one day never quite does; soon you're onto the next thing, and then the next, in a fruitless search for satisfaction.

Mindfulness, despite the high value it places on the moment, is no cousin of live-for-today-forget-tomorrow pleasure-seeking. The contribution it makes is to establish a particular relationship with the present moment; this can bring happiness

Love and friendship

If materialism and pleasure point away from happiness rather than toward it, which way should we travel hopefully? Many people would say that love is their biggest contentment—not a new, romantic kind of love, whose chemistry includes passion and anxiety, but rather the settled kind of love we enjoy with a

TURN LEFT FOR HAPPINESS

In the early 21st century, Dr. Richard Davidson of the University of Wisconsin correlated electrical activity in specific parts of the brain with reported feelings of happiness. His discovery was that positive feelings are accompanied by extra activity in the left prefrontal cortex, and negative feelings in the right prefrontal cortex. The ratio between the two measurements was described as the "mood index." Subsequent work by Dr. Davidson and Jon Kabat-Zinn of the University of Massachusetts Medical School demonstrated that in people who'd undertaken mindfulness training, the readings shifted more to the left. Mindfulness, to put it in unscientific terms, "massages" the brain to be positive about life.

A NEW DIRECTION
Meditation can help to "rewire" the brain to increase our feelings of happiness.

long-term partner, our family, and our friends. Mindfulness, by opening our awareness to the people most precious to us, and encouraging us to understand and express our feelings for them, offers fertile ground for the growth of love. It also offers a form of mindful meditation called loving kindness practice (see pages 138–41), which extends the scope of the heart's remit beyond the narrow circle of our intimates, to people in general, supporting the idea that giving brings rewards to us all.

Purpose and gratitude

People questioned about happiness often speak about purpose—how contentment comes from knowing that they are doing, or at least trying to do, something worthwhile. Mindfulness practice helps you to recognize your true purpose as part of its general enlargement of self-understanding; it also helps you to achieve your goals by sharpening your concentration and decision-making, and building your self-confidence.

Gratitude for what you have is also conducive to happiness, and mindfulness encourages this by exploding the appeal of delusional priorities, such as status, and making you more intensely aware of the gifts of friendship, beauty, and the other riches of your life. Acceptance of what can't be changed is another mindful quality that boosts our sense of well-being.

Happiness under pressure

Everyone finds that their resilience is tested from time to time by misfortune or the consequences of their own mistakes. However, mindfulness promotes resilience because the happiness that it nourishes is not easily compromised. There's often a core of contentment beneath the troubled surface of life's challenges: mindfulness helps you discover it.

OUTGOING HAPPINESS

These words—not arranged in any particular order—make up a checklist, or prompt list, of active ways to bring happiness into your life by involving yourself givingly and mindfully with others.

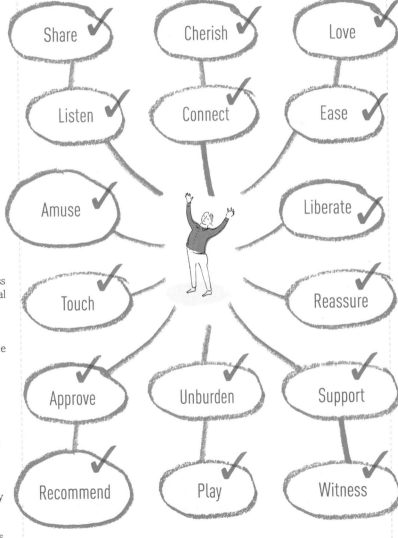

GROWING YOURSELF

MINDFULNESS AND YOUR POTENTIAL

People feel happy when they realize their potential to live as fully and contentedly as circumstances allow. We've seen how mindfulness can contribute to this: here are some further thoughts about breaking down the walls that can block your potential, then choosing your own direction for fulfilment.

Various self-help programs set out to provide tools through which you can realize your potential. They may, for example, encourage you to experiment with new interests or to voice affirmations about your good qualities. Mindfulness is not averse to such techniques, but takes a more coherent approach to self-realization. When you practice mindfulness, you use meditation to shed any negativity in your self-image, replacing that with self-awareness and self-compassion; you then go on to make conscious choices in the light of your priorities.

Inner voices

Sometimes we may fail to realize our full potential because we have an excess of self belief; being over-optimistic about success in a competitive field almost inevitably leads to disappointment. However, we are far more likely to suffer from the opposite delusion—failing to believe enough in ourselves. Negative voices in

ARTIFICIAL CUES FOR FAILURE OR SUCCESS

We often judge ourselves, and set our attitudes and expectations, in response to external cues, which can be positive or negative. Examples of such prompts are given below. Pause to think about their role in setting your mood. Mindfulness helps us keep such prompts in perspective, and see life as a whole.

POSITIVE	NEGATIVE
Praise from others.	Criticism from others.
Good results.	Bad results.
The day starts well.	The day starts badly.
The day ends well.	The day ends badly.
Good news about progress.	Bad news about progress.
Doing more than you expected.	Doing less than you expected.

our heads repeat themselves: "I can't, I can't, I can't." With mindful attention we can be aware of these habitual patterns of thinking and choose, instead, to focus our minds on the authentic reality of present experience. Self-criticism will only hold us back if we engage with it, so we should learn to ignore the voices in our heads, unless they are motivating affirmations we deliberately place there.

Everyday potential

It is easy to get confused about what self-realization really means. It is not the same as achievement, which has overtones of making a public impression—of gaining acclaim or respect among our peers. For example, in weighing up whether to sacrifice their careers for motherhood, many women imagine the domestic sphere to be inferior to the professional. In fact, of course, it's down to personal priorities: for anyone who chooses to be a full-time mother, that course automatically becomes superior.

If we become confused about the meaning of self-realization, mindfulness can clarify our true priorities and prevent our feeling guilty about rejecting other options. It can also

When you practice mindfulness, you use meditation to shed any negativity in your self-image

help us detach ourselves from other peoples' opinions, which are often either too negative or too flattering.

Looking off-center

One of the questions that arises when we consider how to fulfill our potential is where to concentrate our efforts. Should we build strengths or correct weaknesses? The answer needs to come from self-understanding: are we really as clumsy at communication as we feel ourselves to be? Do we really have the aptitude and staying power to retrain in a new profession? Intuition and awareness are key, steering us away from the "funnel effect:" the idea that if we're working to improve in one area, we don't need to spare any energy to work on other issues. Beware of single-mindedness: mindful self-observation scans the whole field of view.

SELF-REALIZATION PREVIEW

To release your true potential, your best course of action is to follow a schedule of mindfulness meditations. The following ideas, expressed as "me"-statements, offer a short preview of what you can expect to believe more confidently as your training progresses:

- I'm entirely myself, not the sum of what other people think about me

- I choose my own priorities in the light of all relevant factors

- I choose my own goals and my criteria for success in reaching those goals

- I'm wary of my expectations but I am fully committed to my intentions

- I know my feelings and choose which ones to act upon

- I change my priorities and my goals when my circumstances change

- I accept what happens to me, without frustration.

Can I really see myself doing an online course in psychology and seeing it through to the end?

Beware of "Can I see myself ...?" That's one of the most limiting thoughts we can have, since we often see ourselves askew.

CONSTRUCTIVE DIALOGUES
The way you express your inner dialogues can build barriers that prevent you from realizing your potential.

MINDFULNESS AND TRADITION
BUDDHIST ROOTS

> We are shaped by our thoughts; we become what we think. When the mind is pure, joy follows like a shadow that never leaves.
>
> The Buddha

Mindfulness has its origins in Buddhism—a belief system that goes back more than 2,000 years. The Buddha's teachings are gathered in ancient scriptures, the *Dhammapada*, one verse of which begins with the idea "Mindfulness is the way to Enlightenment."

Siddhartha Gautama Buddha, usually known simply as the Buddha, spent much of his life spreading his teachings in northern India, sometime between the 6th and 4th centuries BCE.

The Buddha never claimed to be a prophet or a deity, though he had found enlightenment through meditation (Buddha means "the one who is awake") and had gained insight into the meaning of life and the causes of suffering. Just before his death, he appealed to humankind to be mindful and (perhaps less relevant to some of us today), to try to escape the endless cycle of reincarnations. He knew that by cultivating mindfulness we could all become enlightened—not by ideas but by attending to direct experience.

Letting go of attachments
The Buddha wasn't interested in doctrine, and Buddhism isn't exactly a religion. Instead, he attempted to teach humankind a practical way to deal with suffering. This involved training people in how to let go of "attachment," the

illusory things we all cling to, such as pleasure, desire, comfort, and the past—"illusory" because sooner or later they will all fade into nothingness. Clinging to attachments that will

necessarily fade causes all our suffering: by letting go, or "freeing the heart," we can release the mind from illusions that bind us to unhappiness. In the process of becoming more aware and realistic about ourselves and life in general, we attain peace.

To liberate ourselves from desire and find peace as the Buddha taught, we need to know our own minds. Hence the importance of meditation in Buddhism; it is here that we find stillness, and detached from the claims

THE FOUR PILLARS OF MINDFULNESS

The Four Noble Truths are the most basic formulation of the Buddha's teaching:

1 All existence is *dukkha*—"suffering"
2 The cause of *dukkha* is wanting
3 The cessation of *dukkha* comes with the cessation of craving
4 The eightfold path (see above, right) leads to the cessation of suffering.

We can translate these truths into the Four Pillars of Mindfulness: a set of propositions that can save us from error and unhappiness.

> Modern life has its challenges, such as striving for more, or feeling jealousy, which can undermine our well-being.

of the material and the clamor of the emotional we become mindful. The Buddha taught several different forms of meditation designed to build tranquillity and insight, and foster the attributes of compassion, love, and friendship. Such meditations are at the core of mindfulness practice today.

Buddhist mindfulness

The Buddha set out instructions on how to live in the Noble Eightfold Path (see box, right) and said that following this path was the only possible way to attain self-awakening and escape from suffering. The path is eightfold because it requires us to develop eight qualities, including Right Effort and Right Concentration (both references to meditation) as well as Right Mindfulness to develop mentally in the ways that contribute to our liberation. The Buddha also spoke of four distinct forms of mindfulness: of the body, of feelings or sensations, of the mind or mental processes, and of mental objects or qualities. He placed mindfulness practice at the heart of his teachings.

THE WHEEL OF TRUTH

In Buddhism, the Noble Eightfold Path is often represented as the Dharma Wheel, whose eight spokes correspond to the eight elements of the path. "Dharma" is the word used to described the Buddha's teachings, which the Wheel symbolizes.

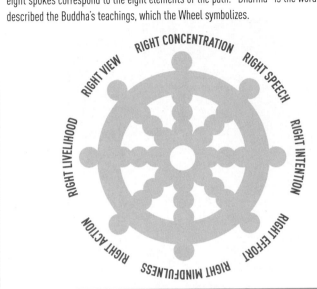

That loss of well-being results from pointlessly wishing things were otherwise—we cling to what we cannot have.

Through mindfulness we can learn to center our well-being in ourselves, making it much less susceptible to changes in external circumstances.

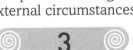

We make our own true choices about our life's path and when challenges do occur, we can face them with awareness.

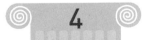

MINDFULNESS FOR HEALTH AND WELL-BEING

MODERN THERAPIES

In the late 20th century, Buddhist-based mindfulness morphed into several new meditation-based approaches to healing. These are grounded in the belief that people can attain some relief from pain or distress by transforming their way of thinking through mindfulness meditation.

The modern history of mindfulness dates from the 1970s and the work of Jon Kabat-Zinn, a molecular scientist and practitioner of meditation. Kabat-Zinn developed a stress reduction program for people suffering from a wide range of chronic medical and psychological conditions, from heart problems to panic attacks. Held at the University of Masschusetts Medical Center, his eight-week course was based on meditation and body awareness, combined with simple yoga postures. Relaunched in 1990 as MBSR, or Mindfulness-Based Stress Reduction, the approach was secular in character despite its roots in Buddhism.

What's right with you?

Kabat-Zinn examined what makes us all tick and our shared sources of distress. He considered the challenges of modern life, as well as age-old problems such as low self-esteem. His emphasis, though, was as much on "what's right with you?" as "what's wrong with you?". He showed that by shifting our focus away from the negative, toward the positive, we can free ourselves from some of the debilitating thoughts and feelings linked with ill-health.

Working on depression

Before long, groups of therapists and researchers began to integrate MBSR with existing psychological therapies, notably Cognitive Behavioral Therapy (CBT). This therapy had been designed to help people with acute depression and is based on the idea that thoughts, feelings, sensations, and actions are interconnected. Negative thoughts and feelings can trap people in a vicious cycle, which the therapist helps to eliminate by dividing large problems into smaller segments, and then

"It's great to see someone transformed in eight weeks from a melancholy, withdrawn person to someone who's receptive and upbeat and can take pleasure in the moment."

Healthcare professional

CLINICAL SUCCESS
Mindfulness-Based Cognitive Therapy has been shown to halve the recurrence of depression in patients who have suffered three or more depressive episodes.

THE BOOK OF CATASTROPHE

Jon Kabat-Zinn wrote a doorstopper-sized book about his mindfulness-based stress reduction methods and the experiences that inspired them and came out of them. The curious title, *Full Catastrophe Living: Using the Wisdom of Your Body and Mind to Face Stress, Pain and Illness* (1990), is derived from a line in the movie *Zorba the Greek*, when Zorba speaks of family life as "the full catastrophe" (see right). The acknowledgment of stress and illness in the title set the tone for many later writers on mindfulness. The preface to the book is by Thich Nhat Hanh, the Vietnamese Zen Buddhist monk with whom Kabat-Zinn had studied Buddhism.

> "Are you married?"
> Basil, an English writer working on a manuscript about the Buddha
>
> "Am I not a man? And is not a man stupid? I'm a man, so I married. Wife, children, house, everything. The full catastrophe."
> Alexis Zorba

showing how to change these negative patterns and feel better as a result. The alliance of CBT and MBSR is called Mindfulness-Based Cognitive Therapy (MBCT), and research shows it to be very effective, particularly in reducing the recurrence of depression.

MBCT works by helping people to understand what depression is—what makes them susceptible to mood spirals, and the reasons they get trapped at the bottom of a spiral. It provides people with a greater awareness of their own bodies, so they can spot signs of oncoming depression. Through mindfulness, they can notice their mood turning downward, and buck the trend, recovering a sense of self-worth.

Many MBCT practitioners also recognize that mindfulness is not just for the ill, but can benefit anyone having difficulty coping with the relentless demands of modern life. It has great potential for helping people build resilience at key periods in their lives, such as having a baby, struggling with life-work balance, or coping with aging.

Flexibility to ACT

While MBSR and MBCT use forms of meditation as their core mindfulness skills, a new therapy—Acceptance and Commitment Therapy (ACT)—focuses on three mental skills—defusion, acceptance, and contact with the here and now. Pioneered by psychologist Steven C. Hayes, ACT helps people achieve psychological flexibility—the ability to be in the present moment, with awareness and openness, and take action, guided by their values.

Shifting our focus away from the negative, toward the positive, we can free ourselves from some of the debilitating thoughts and feelings linked with ill-health.

GOING MAINSTREAM
THE MINDFULNESS REVOLUTION

Mindfulness is spreading fast. The ease with which it can be practiced, together with its proven, wide-ranging benefits for personal effectiveness and well-being, have propelled it into the mainstream in the first two decades of the 21st century.

Any self-help discipline that's promoted as a way to increase our chances of happiness has a good chance of taking root—especially when it comes with evidence-based research to show it can also make us feel better about ill-health and less likely to fall prey to stress. Add to that the dimension of personal effectiveness—the improvement of concentration, memory, communication, and emotional self-control—and you can see why mindfulness is a flourishing movement.

Jon Kabat-Zinn has said that mindfulness practice is beneficial precisely because we don't strive toward particular goals: we "befriend ourselves as we are," hanging out with ourselves in awareness. Yet it is the particular gains that mindfulness brings that have endeared it to the leading lights of business and public life. Google's "Search Inside Yourself" program, started in 2007, introduced mindfulness to more than 1,000 of the company's employees, and similar initiatives have been taken by Silicon Valley entrepreneurs, Fortune 500 titans, Pentagon chiefs, and many others.

Mindfulness at work
The blend of promoting happiness and personal effectiveness has proven especially attractive to employers, who have found that offering mindfulness training within the workplace has benefitted their employees and themselves. The employers' gain is twofold. Mindfulness hones people's skills, making them more focused, better able to juggle priorities, solve problems, cooperate in teams, lead others, and be creative. Gains are achieved in innovation and efficiency. But in addition, a happier worker is a more productive worker, and is more likely to stay with the company and show loyalty.

> "Stress reduction and mindfulness don't just make us happier and healthier, they're a proven competitive advantage for any business."
>
> Arianna Huffington, founder of the *Huffington Post*

A MINDFUL WORLD
Mindfulness has spread from its origins in Buddhism to therapeutic settings and the spheres of business, education, and sports, where its application has had measurable benefits.

Business schools, too, have embraced the practice. Bill George, the former boss of Medtronic, a global medical technology company, and a board member at investment bank Goldman Sachs, introduced mindfulness at Harvard Business School in an attempt to develop leaders who are "self-aware and self-compassionate."

The connection between mindfulness practice and training for leadership was strengthened with the publication in 2011 of *The Three Levels of Leadership*, a new model for professional development by UK business coach, James Scouller. This system, which emphasizes psychological self-mastery, includes mindfulness meditation as one of its main self-development tools.

Beyond business, mindfulness has taken its message into government and public services. James Scouller has presented his methods to cadets at Sandhurst, the college where British Army officers are trained, and US Armed Forces personnel benefit from mindfulness training in their "Coping Strategies" program.

In prisons, mindfulness has been employed effectively to reduce hostility and mood disturbance among inmates and to improve self-esteem. And in schools, both teachers and pupils are reaping the benefits of mindfulness: some principals believe that the decline in religious assemblies has created a hole in school life—the loss of a daily opportunity for quiet reflection that mindfulness sessions can fill.

Sports performance

Mindfulness has also been adopted in some sporting circles. Research with golfers, runners, and archers report improvements in performance and a rise in rankings among practitioners. Using mindfulness meditations such as the body scan (see pages 118–23), athletes reported feeling "in the zone"— completely absorbed in their actions and experiences. Performance benefits included better concentration, feeling "effortless," reduced self-consciousness, and a heightened sense of mastery.

STEVE JOBS AND THE BUSINESS ENLIGHTENMENT

Mindfulness practice in business was not a wild idea that came from nowhere. Eastern mysticism had already nourished a number of business leaders who cared about the well-being of their companies and employees, and sought to create an enlightened business culture. Steve Jobs, Apple's founder and former chief executive, was a Zen Buddhist, and reported how his beliefs fed into Apple product design. Jobs spoke to his biographer, Walter Isaacson, about the importance of just sitting and observing, and the way that enables you to notice your restless mind. Then calm is achieved, and with that comes a more refined intuition. When the mind slows down, you see, as he put it, "an expanse in the moment."

THE MINDFUL ZEITGEIST

THE POWER TO TRANSFORM SOCIETY

Mindfulness is already effective at an individual and organizational level, but some influential business analysts see a greater potential. They say that mindfulness is capable of changing the way society works at a number of levels.

I magine a world in which mindfulness practice was a part of everyday life, and where it was fully integrated into society. What might the benefits be? Reduced spending on healthcare? Higher achievement levels in schools? Improved economic productivity? It is hard to predict, but decision-makers are taking such ideas seriously. In 2014, for example, a parliamentary group was set up in the UK to study how to bring mindfulness into public policy. Also in 2014, mindfulness was identified in a report by J. Walter Thompson (JWT)—one of the world's largest communications companies—as one of ten trends set to shape societal mood, attitudes, and behavior. Not only was mindfulness significant in itself, but it could exert a profound influence on the other trends shaping our lives (see right).

> "Now we're trying to be more mindful ... and find more balance."
>
> Ann Mack, JWT

1
WRAPAROUND EXPERIENCES
We're seeing the rise of immersive entertainment—narratives and brand experiences that work on many levels, using mixed media. An example would be movies shown in elaborate special settings, with interactive audience involvement. Sensory overload of this kind could be read as intellectually demeaning: it implies that many of us are unable to take enjoyment any more in less lavish, more traditional forms of entertainment.

2
IMPERFECTIONISM
Frustrated with commercial spin and the glossy surfaces loved by the retail sector, as well as by affluent consumers, many are taking refuge in authentic imperfection. This is seen in a return to home crafts and in reuse of old materials—which, of course, has an ecological dimension too. Since mindfulness values authenticity of the self, many practitioners are likely to carry this through into their surroundings and support imperfectionism. We're all imperfect, and accepting our flaws is the mindful way.

3
THE NEW TECHNO-SCEPTICISM
Seeing our children addicted to digital devices, and suffering ourselves from information overload, many of us are drawn to a counterrevolution, based on prioritizing human values. Face-to-face meetings are being championed in business. Since mindfulness favors direct experience, rather than secondhand experience, many converts to mindfulness will have serious reservations about the digital revolution.

4
INSTANT SATISFACTION

The time lag between ask and receive, and want and enjoy, is getting shorter, with the rise of the on-demand economy, impatience with download speeds, and so on. The Internet accelerates the process of choice, as well as the delivery of what you've chosen—waiting is so last year! Mindfulness, however, trains us in patience, and teaches us to find pleasure in modest experiences unconnected with the gratification of our desires.

8
MARKET MIND-READING

With the development of brain–computer interfaces and emotion recognition technology, brands are getting smarter at understanding how consumers think and behave, and marketing to them in a highly personalized way. Many will find it uncomfortable, even infuriating, to have their needs interpreted on the basis of past behavior: it's far from mindful.

6
SMARTPHONE POWER

Smartphones are extending their dominion, providing people with access to financial systems, personal health monitoring... and even mindful meditations. There's nothing wrong with such developments in themselves, but to hitch our pleasures too much to the latest phone technology, and indeed to be emotionally dependent on it, is an example of misplaced priorities—and, in Buddhist terms, the kind of "attachment" that will never bring true contentment, only the illusion of it.

JWT'S TEN TRENDS TO SHAPE OUR WORLD

9
IMAGE VS. WORD

Visual language, in the form of graphics, emoticons, and the like, seems to be eroding the time-honored power of the word. This is partly to do with globalization, because it provides a way to reach a worldwide market without the burden of translation. However, for communicating subtle meanings, which mindfulness trains us to appreciate, the image is a much cruder tool than the word.

7
THE END OF PRIVACY

New technologies make it more difficult for us to avoid being the object of surveillance by private and public organizations. For some, this a moral battlefield: individuals hate being snooped on, and libertarians object to loss of privacy rights even when it's arguably in the interests of security. Mindful people will make their own judgement about this: some will mind more than others.

5
MINDFUL LIVING

JWT recognizes that mindfulness, once associated with people seeking spiritual fulfillment, is now filtering into the mainstream, with more and more attracted by the idea of blocking out distractions and attending to the moment. Of course, people follow trends for different reasons. Some, thinking mindfulness is "cool," will gravitate toward an attractive social set. But many will be genuinely looking for ways to bring well-being and happiness into their lives; and many too will be trying to find relief from stress and anxiety, and the pressures of modern living.

10
CULTURAL MIX AND MATCH

Cultural mixing within Western societies, and the pick-and-choose culture fostered by the Internet, are encouraging people to create their own blends of beliefs and practices, mixing traditional elements with more recent, or even wholly invented ideas. Since modern mindfulness itself fuses old and new, with elements from different sciences and a great deal of experiment, it's hard to imagine mindfulness practitioners objecting to such tendencies.

TOWARD A MINDFUL YOU

BY UNDERSTANDING HOW THOUGHTS AND EMOTIONS INTERACT, AND HOW THEY OFTEN STEM FROM THE PAST, WE CAN HUGELY ENRICH OUR POTENTIAL.

WHAT DO YOU THINK YOU'RE LIKE?
MINDFULNESS AND PERSONALITY

We all have characteristics that make us unique: this is our personality. If we view our personality traits as tendencies, not patterns, we're less likely to be limited by them. The mindful approach is to get to know ourselves, and use that knowledge to make choices.

Psychologists love to classify, and in the past, studies of personality tended to focus on categorizing people into universal "types." Such assessments have fallen out of favor, though we still come across them in various forms, especially in the business world, when assessing contributions to teamwork.

Shades of gray
Psychologists now speak of traits more than types—a more useful and less reductive approach. For example, we can try to pinpoint our position on a scale between introversion and extraversion—terms that date back to a book by Swiss psychologist Carl Jung, published in 1921. Jung represented these qualities as an absolute pairing: you were either one thing or the other. In fact, no one is wholly extravert (outward) or introvert (inward), and studies by the German psychologist Hans Eysenck and others have shown that most people are in fact a balanced mixture of the two, albeit with a preference in one direction. Another popular scale of assessment, derived from Jung's contrast of thinking and feeling, runs from something like "tough-minded" to "sympathetic."

Exploring personality
The emphasis of mindfulness is to realize your potential and bring to light your true options. The true mindful self is found in the unfolding of thoughts, emotions, and actions, so if you think of yourself as a fixed personality type, such as introverted or sympathetic, then you are living in the past, not in the present, and you limit your scope for positive change.

It is, however, possible to use personality traits as a tool for mindful self-discovery. Think about the adjectives associated with personality traits and consider whether you might have appeared—in the past—to have shown these characteristics in your behavior toward others. Do any of these words chime with how you sometimes describe yourself? Think about these views of your self with mindful attention; this process can help you examine your strengths and weaknesses. Mindfulness will help you to approach such self-assessments honestly and carefully. By avoiding judgement, and considering the questions in the moment, you're more likely to come up with useful responses that are true to your experience.

The Big Five
An interesting starting point for self-exploration might be the well-known set of Big Five personality traits (see right). Use the diagram to think about your position on the five scales: openness, conscientiousness, extraversion, agreeableness, and sensitivity (also called neuroticism).

Personality types, though never a good excuse, help you understand and forgive your own behavior. But beware of using them to stereotype yourself.

THE BIG FIVE WORD CUES

The Big Five personality traits are a synthesis of psychologists' attempts to name the entire range of human attitudes and behavior. Accepting the shortcomings of this listing, you can still use it as a cue for self-discovery. Scan the word scales for each category; if neither extreme in the scales is a word you'd use to describe yourself, see if you can think of a word, falling somewhere on the scale, that would. Experiment to spin off further self-descriptive words with similar meanings.

OPENNESS

Curious ⟷ Convinced
Experimental ⟷ Selective
Creative ⟷ Consolidating
Imaginative ⟷ Logical
Independent ⟷ Consistent

CONSCIENTIOUSNESS

Responsible ⟷ Relaxed
Dutiful ⟷ Self-motivated
Careful ⟷ Spontaneous
Meticulous ⟷ Decisive
Perfectionist ⟷ Self-tolerant

SENSITIVITY

Optimistic ⟷ Questioning
Resilient ⟷ Empathetic
Confident ⟷ Tentative
Inspiring ⟷ Impressionable
Trusting ⟷ Watchful

EXTRAVERSION

Assertive ⟷ Flexible
Energetic ⟷ Calm
Sociable ⟷ Self-contained
Talkative ⟷ Contemplative
Expressive ⟷ Reticent

AGREEABLENESS

Compassionate ⟷ Implacable
Cooperative ⟷ Sceptical
Compromising ⟷ Determined
Amenable ⟷ Resolute
Responsive ⟷ Composed

DISPOSED TOWARD THE MOMENT

ARE YOU NATURALLY MINDFUL?

Do you enjoy listening to what people have to say? Do you make quality time for your partner or children? You may be "dispositionally mindful" with an existing measure of mindfulness in your psychological makeup. If so, you are likely to take to mindfulness meditation like a duck to water.

Mindfulness is a technique but it's also a personality trait (though not recognized as one of the Big Five, see page 39). If self-awareness comes to you readily and you already tend to inspect your thoughts, sensations, and emotions on a regular basis, you're predisposed to be mindful. Scientific studies have shown that people who are dispositionally mindful respond better to stress, and are less susceptible to negative mood states than others; they have better cardiovascular health; and some (though not all) of their cognitive functions are enhanced. Other research has indicated that dispositional mindfulness may be encouraged by aerobic exercise, although more work needs to be done before this can be stated with certainty.

DISPOSED TO BE MINDFUL
If you prefer simple pleasures to striving, you may be dispositionally mindful.

Mindfulness is an inner spotlight that you can direct on yourself at any moment for the purpose of self-discovery.

Whether you are innately mindful or not, practicing mindfulness through meditation builds on your preexisting human capabilities. If you think of mindfulness as an inner spotlight that you can direct toward yourself at any moment for the purpose of self-discovery, then meditation helps to make that spotlight brighter and more focused.

It's important at this point to distinguish between self-awareness and self-absorption. Many people think and talk frequently about their inner life, and in particular their emotions. Emotional intelligence is valued highly today, and those who aspire to it often understand that it needs to be grounded in empathy—that is, the ability to put yourself in another person's situation, and to identify with what they're feeling. This in turn requires that you have a good appreciation of your own feelings. Unfortunately, many introspective people, who would claim to be emotionally intelligent, may sometimes come up with inaccurate observations about their own feelings: they shine the spotlight on the right place but not with true illumination.

Body language
It's been said that the one thing we don't know about ourselves is the thing that other people know only too well. It's possible to think of yourself as confident, for example, while in fact

MINDFUL TEMPERAMENT CHECKLIST

To help you assess your level of predispositional mindfulness, ask yourself which of the following statements apply to you. The more you check off, the more likely it is you have a mindful temperament, although there's nothing systematic about the list: for more rigorous self-testing, do the questionnaires later in this chapter.

- ✓ You're seldom surprised when people make comments about your strengths or your weaknesses.

- ✓ When feeling anxious, your first step is to try to separate yourself from your anxiety and look at it from the outside.

- ✓ When feeling angry, the first thing you do is spend several seconds trying to clear your head before saying or doing anything.

- ✓ You could list, if asked, a number of regular habitual reaction patterns that you're prone to experience in certain situations.

- ✓ When thinking about past or future events, you sometimes stop yourself and consciously return to the present.

- ✓ You often respond with gratitude, pleasure, or wonder to positive events you observe around you.

- ✓ You don't fight it when good things in your life come to an end, since you know it's beyond your control.

MINDFUL MARKERS
Analyzing your behavior, your emotional responses, and your attitudes to people helps gauge your level of dispositional mindfulness.

being rather anxious in company. You can't necessarily detect what messages your own body language is conveying, whereas the people in the room with you will detect your anxiety from the high pitch of your voice, or the way your eyes dart about, or your hands fiddle with your bag. Those predisposed to be mindful are unlikely to miss such symptoms. They'll be aware of themselves and be able to identify the kinds of situation that tend to make them uncomfortable. They might even be able to detach themselves from their discomfort, at least sometimes.

WHEEL AND COMPASS

DOING AND BEING MINDS

The mind is a wonderfully versatile instrument for steering us through the day. It can also be a compass, providing readings to help us navigate by. But often it forgets to take its bearings, making our voyage a turbulent one.

As you have breakfast, perhaps between snatches of family talk, you think ahead to what the day holds for you. You picture events and wonder how they'll go. You'll be hopeful about some, anxious about others; some will be neutral—you'll simply be reminding yourself that you have to make time for an errand or to follow up a task at work. Meanwhile, you're engaging with a child or partner. While chatting you remember something else on your to-do list. For many people, especially those with young families, this is a very familiar scenario.

Breakfast of doing

During breakfast, you've been doing and thinking at the same time, but much of the thinking was restless. Your mind was in "doing" mode propelled by a succession of thoughts, recollections, desires, and problems. Now imagine another scenario. Your family are away, and you're enjoying a solo mini-vacation at home. With time

SIGNS OF THE "DOING" MODE

We're operating in "doing" mode whenever we're not simply being. This checklist—with examples—will help you recognize some categories of the "doing" mode.

Wondering if you've said or done the right thing.

JUDGEMENT
Measuring what happens, or has happened, against what "should" have happened.

Thinking that you should be more tolerant, proactive, or productive.

SELF-CRITICISM
Taking a critical stance in your inner dialogue with yourself—berating yourself for your errors.

Deciding whether to sell your house, or go to the store, or how to cheer up a friend.

PROBLEM-SOLVING AND DECIDING
Working out what action to take, and tracing the possible consequences of that action.

to yourself, you enjoy a quiet breakfast, reading the newspaper. You're going to do some gardening later. In the middle of an article, your mind for no reason starts dwelling on work. How will they manage without you? Should you have told your assistant you're getting a bit restless in the company? Will she tell somebody else? Then you decide you've spent long enough thinking about work—you're supposed to be relaxing, after all. Pity it's only for three days. Or is it four? Then you decide to visit the garden center, to buy some plants for that difficult shady border. What might grow there?

Relaxed isn't mindful

Despite the relaxed circumstances and your expectation of quiet "me time" during your mini-vacation, your mind is once again in "doing" mode in which one thought leads to the next. What's more, you are being carried along with it. Some of your thoughts are reflective, some are decisions to take action, but there's still no

What if I hadn't let that tree grow so high? Would I now have lots of sun-loving plants?

Are you wondering or regretting? "What if" is often "If only" in disguise.

THE WHEEL TURNS
Self-criticism and constant analysis of your decisions are signs of a mind locked in "doing."

mindfulness here. Your autopilot might be happily chugging along, and even giving some enjoyment, but it's autopilot nevertheless.

Choiceless awareness

The alternative mind mode to "doing" is "being." You find yourself worrying about work over breakfast, but you don't chastise yourself for these worries or switch your attention to the future

("Is it four days or three?"). Instead, you shift into "being" mode. You direct your attention to the present moment, observing your thoughts and worries without getting drawn into their content. You bring a gentle awareness to yourself and your true feelings. This is how you can let go of the "doing" mode and move into the "being" mode—the compass—where you can become aware of your true direction.

Feeling angry with your neighbor and wondering how he could have been so thoughtless.

ENGAGING WITH FEELINGS
Inhabiting emotions, and reliving the narrative behind them.

Recalling the last time you enjoyed yourself so much, or reminiscing about a romantic evening.

REMEMBERING
Taking your mind back to the past, whether anxiously, regretfully, pleasurably, or with any other emotion.

Wondering if there'll be refreshments at a party, or wondering if your home insurance would cover you if you broke your glasses.

SPECULATING
Taking your mind into the future, whether anxiously, hopefully, or with pleasurable anticipation.

Protesting on hearing someone telling a lie, or giving someone a hug when they start crying.

REACTING
Showing involuntary reactions to experiences rather than pausing to consider your response.

ALIVE IN THE PRESENT
MOVING INTO BEING

Taking a step back in our minds from doing and instead moving into a state of pure, present being is a key skill of mindfulness. Attending to our sensations, thoughts, and feelings means that the negative energies in our minds lose much of their influence.

The mind's "doing" mode is the mode of efficiency—the realm in which we get things done in the physical world. We have seen that this mode has its negative aspects—it is here that we react automatically, worry about the future, and regret the past—but it offers up so many possibilities for moving toward our personal goals. In comparison, the "being" mode may seem rather dull and unappealing: after all, what's the point of just sitting there, with a still mind, unless you're a mystic or a Buddhist in a deep state of absorbed concentration?

Dropping into being
The "being" mode is not just for the spiritually minded: the basic, non-judging (or choiceless) awareness that comes to the foreground when you drop into "being" mode has been a vital inner resource from the start of our conscious lives, and it's available to us at every moment. It can give us nourishment and calm within our busy lives of seemingly endless doing. What we gain from this is not spiritual wisdom but a practical way to inhabit our everyday lives more fully.

The challenge of being
When you combine the "being" mode with noticing your sensations, thoughts, or feelings, you enter a mindful state, with its attendant physical and psychological benefits. Achieving that state takes practice; if you just try "being" for a few seconds, you won't find it easy. You're in the middle of following a train of thought, which your mind won't want to abandon.

So what does "being" look like? This thought experiment will give you an idea. Imagine that you're sitting in the park, looking intently at a rose. You let go of everything in your mind except the sensation of the rose; there's room in your thoughts for past or future, for anxiety, or for any other emotion. If a thought intrudes, you simply let it drift out of your mind in the same way that it drifted in. You don't battle with that thought because that would take you back into the doing mode. You have chosen mindfulness.

> What should I do if an emotion or distracting thought suddenly pops into my head?

> Simply observe it, without engaging with it, without judging it, without doing anything with it at all.

DEALING WITH INTRUDERS
In a mindful state, thoughts and emotions are neither welcome nor unwelcome.

SIGNS OF THE "BEING" MODE

Get to know the characteristics of the "being" mode through this checklist; compare its features with those of the "doing" mode on page 42. Notice that it is in the nature of the being mode that many of its features are expressed in the negative. Use this list when you look back on your first attempts at just being, to see whether your thinking attained any of these qualities, or non-qualities.

NON-JUDGEMENT
Not measuring what happens or has happened against what should be happening or should have happened. "Should" thinking has no place here.

LIVING IN THE MOMENT
"Being here now" and not engaging with any thought of past or future that happens to come into your mind.

ACCEPTANCE
Not engaging in a critical or disappointed dialogue with yourself, and being compassionate with yourself whenever you unintentionally think of any kind of error you've made.

ATTENTION
Focusing the mind on its own experience in the moment and, if it gets distracted, gently returning your focus to the object of your attention.

PASSIVITY
Not making decisions, planning, or problem-solving: these all belong to the "doing" mode.

RESPONSIVENESS
Not reacting to any unwanted inner or outer distractions (thoughts or sensations), but simply noticing them and letting them drift away.

NONENGAGEMENT
Not getting absorbed into an emotion or unwanted thought that happens to cross your mind; remaining distant from an emotion's underlying story.

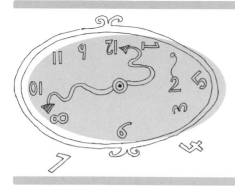

TIME WARPS
STUCK IN THE PAST, ANXIOUS ABOUT THE FUTURE?

Our true home is the present. This is the only place where our lives are actually occurring. Learning to live mindfully in the here and now will make us more grounded, more balanced, and happier.

We learn from the past—our treasury of memories and source of emotional support—while thinking about the future may spur optimism, determination, and ambition. Even so, it isn't good for us to spend too long in these places: mindfulness can reground our attention in the present.

The power of the past
Our past is made up of things we have experienced, and some of these experiences may have been bad ones. Someone might have might harmed us,

making us wary in the present, or we might have done something we deeply regret. Many present anxieties have roots in our past, even if we're unable to trace them.

We can't change the past, so we may try to make up for mistakes by denying ourselves pleasures or trying to do now what we failed to do before. However sincere these attempts, we may find life is overshadowed by guilt or regret, dragging our thoughts back to the past and limiting our chances of happiness in the present.

Anybody home?

The answer is, not always; and in fact, not often enough.

BE IN THE MOMENT
We spend too long in the past and future, failing to attend to the present.

If guilt is a complaint against ourselves, the past is often a cause of complaints against others. Anger is easily revived by memories of past wrongs, surging in fresh aggression; while resentment "simmers," with low-level hostility.

Through mindfulness you can harness the positive power of the present to change your relationship with the past. No pitched battle is necessary. The present has merely to be attended to, and the power of past events will fade away.

> The past, if we can't come to terms with it, can breed guilty or resentful feelings, while the future is an imagined prospect that may fill us with anxiety.

JAILBREAK!

Imprisoned in guilt or shame, we need mindfulness to plan our great escape. The key is to learn how to stop judging ourselves (see p16). It's only our distorted perception, and more specifically our lack of self-compassion, that makes a prison of the past. The cell we're locked in is of our own making and mindfulness meditation gives us the key. When we give attention to the present moment the past releases us from captivity. With the key in our hands, mindfully we unlock the door and walk free.

THE PRISON BARS OF GUILT

Being a poor son, daughter, or parent.

Being a poor partner.

Being unable to cope.

Being unable to succeed.

Being selfish.

THE PRISON BARS OF SHAME

Failing to excel.

Failing to control your emotions.

Failing to be responsible.

Failing to be normal.

Failing to fit in.

FINDING THE KEY
We already possess the key to escape the prison of our past.

QUESTIONNAIRE: TIME TRAVELER

HOW WELL DO YOU KNOW THE PRESENT?

The questions here are prompts for self-exploration. Given the perils of dwelling too much on the past and the future, and the benefits of inhabiting the present, the answers you give should prompt you to think about what tendencies you need to work on with the help of mindfulness practice.

Q Mind in the past?

- How often do you go over past events in your mind?
- Are there specific events in your past that still trouble you today?
- How anxious does it make you to think about your worst mistakes?
- How angry does it make you feel when you think about the worst things people have said or done to you?

Q Mind in the present?

- How observant do you think you are as you move around your neighborhood?
- How strong are your powers of concentration?
- How often does your mind tend to wander when you settle down to concentrate on music?
- How often have you valued a walk for the sights and sounds of nature more than for the opportunity to talk with a companion or think things through?

Q Mind in the future?

- How often do you look forward to future pleasures, imagining what they will be like?
- How many specific events in the future make you anxious when you think about them?
- How positive do you feel when you think about the most enjoyable experience the immediate future holds for you?
- How negative do you feel when you think about the most unenjoyable experience the immediate future holds for you?

ARE YOU AWARE OF YOUR SURROUNDINGS?

The expression "He/she walks around in a daze" is often heard. In fact, most of us, outside and inside the home, inhabit the daze of our own thoughts, and fail to notice the detail of our surroundings. Even when we're walking around, using equipment, talking, and generally going about our business, we give little of our attention to our physical environment. How much do you notice? It's worth looking around properly from time to time: you might notice something useful or interesting.

■ Think about a complicated place you regularly visit and would say you know well—perhaps a shopping mall or an office, or a neighborhood of the city. Sketch a map of the place on a large sheet of paper, and add in as much detail as you can.

■ Write in any names you can remember—for example, the names of stores, or rooms, or streets.

■ List any sequences you can remember—for example, the doors along a corridor, or the stores along a street.

■ Next time you visit the place, walk around with more attention than usual—more mindfully—and test yourself again afterward, perhaps the same day or some time in the future. Did you do better this time?

■ You could also apply this exercise to parts of your own home—for example, the contents of your refrigerator or kitchen pantry. You might discover that even furniture and ornaments are not as familiar to you as you might have expected. Work toward a fuller acquaintance of your immediate surroundings, and gradually progress outward from that.

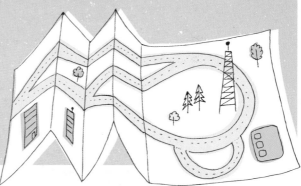

Q Have you visited the now?

■ How often have you experienced being "in the zone"—that is, being so absorbed in what you are doing that you don't notice the passage of time?

■ How often have you noticed changes in the places you regularly visit—such as a new store opening, or a house being painted?

■ When you listen to an interesting speech or someone talking on the TV or radio, what percentage of the words do you think you take in?

EXPLORE FURTHER

If this unsystematic but wide-ranging questionnaire gets you reflecting on your attitude to past, present, and future events, it will have served its purpose. Look at your answers and see if you can detect any propensities or habits you'd like to modify—perhaps you feel they are affecting your level of contentment? Resolve to take note whenever you find yourself thinking about past events or anticipating the future. What moods do you experience when you do this? Get to know your relationship with time.

"To be in harmony with the wholeness of things is to not have anxiety over our imperfections."

Dogen Zenji (1200–1253)

LIFTING THE LID
LETTING GO OF NEGATIVE THOUGHTS AND FEELINGS

We are all capable of thinking positively. What sometimes holds us back are our old habits of thought and feeling, some with roots in the distant past. Understanding what magnifies these bad habits and what's capable of weakening them is an important step in our mindfulness journey.

Most of us know individuals who seem spontaneous, immersed in the world, and who spread energy wherever they go. In their presence, we may even feel a kind of awakening, a call to action, and feel that our own responses to the world are more sluggish than theirs.

These people appear so much more engaged because they have successfully turned down their autopilot. We've seen how autopilot can dull us to the potential for experience offered, and blunt our potential for inner growth, giving us a vague sense of dissatisfaction or staleness.

Auto thoughts
If you're having negative thoughts about yourself, such as "This is beyond my capabilities," "Why should I think it's going to be better this time?" or "Nobody will thank me for doing this," negative emotions will almost inevitably follow in their wake. This thought-plus-emotion pairing

will soon get ingrained in your mind as a pattern—a reflex that impacts on your mood whenever certain kinds of situations recur.

What results is a feedback loop: you believe the voice inside you that says you're useless, because that's how you feel; and you feel that way on account of your inner voice. Such deep patterns

of thinking and feeling whittle away at your well-being, subtly and not always noticeably, until one day you realize how low, irritable, or fatigued you are. All this happens so automatically you don't even realize you have a choice in the matter.

It doesn't have be this way. We all have rights of refusal when it comes to negative thoughts: we don't have

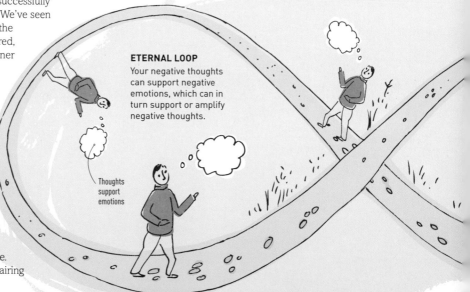

ETERNAL LOOP
Your negative thoughts can support negative emotions, which can in turn support or amplify negative thoughts.

Thoughts support emotions

to believe them, even if it's impossible, at least initially, to keep them, and the emotions that tag along with them, out of our heads. What we need to turn off the inner mechanism of negativity is mindfulness meditation. We may not be able to get rid of negative thoughts but we can learn to treat them with accepting curiosity and shift our relationship with them, taking them less seriously.

Not controlling

If you want to rid yourself of negative patterns of thought and emotion, willful control rarely works. Deciding you're going to resist the thoughts and feelings involved in the complex chemistry of low esteem, hopelessness, and disappointment will only bring further tension. You cannot defeat such problems by putting a lid on them, and containment only makes the pressure build up further—an idea expressed succinctly by Carl Gustav Jung: "What we resist, persists."

If you can't contain an explosion, the obvious approach is to stand back from it. Mindfulness does this, though without any sense of running away.

KEEPING A MINDFULNESS JOURNAL

Practicing mindfulness is a highly subjective experience. The thoughts you have, the things you learn about yourself, and the unconscious mental habits that you uncover are all intensely personal and often fleeting. For some people, recording their experiences in a journal is a very useful exercise because it helps to objectify their thoughts, sensations, and emotions, so that they can be used to refine their meditation in future. A journal can record when you practiced, for how long, and what type of meditation you carried out, so providing markers of your progress.

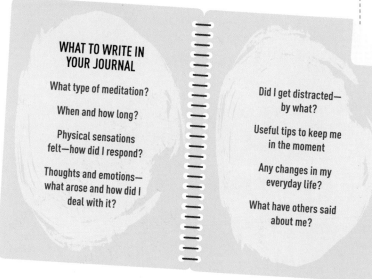

WHAT TO WRITE IN YOUR JOURNAL

What type of meditation?

When and how long?

Physical sensations felt—how did I respond?

Thoughts and emotions—what arose and how did I deal with it?

Did I get distracted—by what?

Useful tips to keep me in the moment

Any changes in my everyday life?

What have others said about me?

BE HONEST
Try to write in your journal every day. Record whatever information or observations you find useful. There's no right or wrong about what to write in the journal, other than the need to be completely honest.

Emotions amplify thoughts

We may not be able to get rid of negative thoughts entirely but we can treat them with accepting curiosity.

CAN'T HELP IT!
WHY HABITS TAKE TIME TO BREAK

Deep-rooted habits can be a block to happiness. While practicing mindfulness meditation is the most effective way to dissolve the force of habit, we can make a start by bringing compassionate attention to our habits and increasing our self-understanding.

It can feel at times as if our lives are living us, rather than we are living our lives. Autopilot, as we've seen, takes our choices away from us without our consent.

Bad habits are reactions to situations, laid down in your body and mind like the rings in a tree trunk. To be reactive is to think, act, or feel instantaneously without allowing yourself a moment to let the situation sink in. As a result, a reflex that's developed over time, and has become as ingrained as a tree's rings, repeats itself without your having a say in the matter. Each occasion on which this happens reinforces the pattern; habits get stronger over time.

Mindfulness gives us the tools to recognize habitual thoughts and reactions, and let them pass through consciousness without effect. With mindfulness meditation we can start to get our choices back, but we need to be persistent with our practice once we've begun, since habit will always try to reassert itself.

WHEN HABIT TAKES THE LEAD

Here are some examples of habitual, autopilot reaction—they are likely to seem familiar. Try thinking of more examples from your own life.

- You meet someone who disliked you at school, and find that you're unable to respond to their friendly overtures

- You believe you're no good at public speaking, and you panic when asked to make a speech at work

- You feel yourself getting tongue-tied when talking to your daughter's teacher, because you know she's very smart and you feel inferior.

Our brain chemistry is changed by our repetitive behaviors, but we don't need to be enslaved by our habits. With mindfulness, we can break free.

Can't I defeat habit simply by saying "no"? Why do I need a program of mindfulness meditation?

PAUSE, THEN PLAY
Mindfulness helps us to widen the gap between stimulus and response, giving us more control.

Mindfulness lets you pause and notice your impulses.

CHART YOUR GOOD AND BAD HABITS

To improve your awareness of how autopilot and involuntary habits affect your life, try charting your habits—both good and bad. Make a note of which negative habits are most entrenched, and which habits you consider positive—those you might wish to keep. Use the template below as a prompt for your thoughts and write your thoughts and feelings in your mindfulness journal (see page 53). You can return to this record as you progress through your mindfulness meditation practice to gauge your progress.

BAD HABITS

DOING

What things do I often do that make me unhappy?

- **On my own**
- **In my family**
- **In my friendships**
- **In my relationships**
- **At work**

Does one of these things happen in all the five areas of life listed above?

THINKING

What thoughts do I have that make me unhappy?

- **About myself**
- **About my family**
- **About my friends**
- **About my relationships**
- **About work**

Does one of these thoughts attach itself to all five areas of life listed above?

EMOTION

What emotions do I often have that make me unhappy?

- **About myself**
- **About my family**
- **About my friends**
- **About my relationships**
- **About work**

Does one of these emotions occur in all five areas of life listed above?

Use the emotions checklist below to help you name your feelings as precisely as possible.

- **Confusion**
- **Frustration**
- **Irritation**
- **Disappointment**
- **Anger**
- **Envy**
- **Jealousy**
- **Oppression**
- **Impatience**
- **Grievance**
- **Helplessness**
- **Hopelessness**
- **Claustrophobia**
- **Bewilderment**
- **Boredom**

GOOD HABITS

DOING

What things do I often do that make me happy?

- **On my own**
- **In my family**
- **In my friendships**
- **In my relationships**
- **At work**

Does one of these things happen in all the five areas of life listed above?

THINKING

What thoughts do I have that make me happy?

- **About myself**
- **About my family**
- **About my friends**
- **About my relationships**
- **About work**

Does one of these thoughts attach itself to all five areas of life listed above?

EMOTION

What emotions do I often have that make me happy?

- **About myself**
- **About my family**
- **About my friends**
- **About my relationships**
- **About work**

Does one of these emotions occur in all five areas of life listed above?

Use the emotions checklist below to help you name your feelings as precisely as possible.

- **Contentment**
- **Gratitude**
- **Love**
- **Patience**
- **Admiration**
- **Pride**
- **Excitement**
- **Inspiration**
- **Pleasure**
- **Happiness**
- **Calm**

LOOSENING HABIT'S GRIP
TOWARD A MORE AUTHENTIC YOU

You can only dislodge deep-seated habits of thinking and feeling over time—and particularly with a course of mindfulness meditation. You can prepare for this by making changes to some of your unproductive *outer* habits—the things you do routinely, unquestioningly.

W e're exposed every day to a countless flow of phenomena— things we hear, read, observe, or perceive in other ways. Much of this information could be useful, suggesting new options for us to take up, or new paths to follow—if only we were willing to attend to it. By a process known as "selective perception," we filter out stimuli that don't fit into our image of our own lives. From time to time it pays to pull back and take in a wider-angle view of the world. We might then see more fulfilling options that are available

and that could help us lead fuller lives. To realize our potential is, in part, to say goodbye to false identities and live more authentically, finding our true selves.

Keeping busy
One of the habits many of us have is keeping endlessly busy, throwing ourselves into action to avoid making time for contemplation. Unconsciously, we fear that introspection might force us to face uncomfortable truths about ourselves. Work, in particular, provides

> Ignoring things you dislike can be a limiting habit. Keep a little ambivalence in your life—your mind will be more open and your experiences more interesting.

a compelling distraction. We stay late at the office, telling ourselves that we need to put in the hours to compete with colleagues, or to impress the boss, but in truth so much of our identity is tied up with work that we'd feel lost without it.

FIVE HABIT-LOOSENERS

Here are five simple ways to move toward a more authentic self. Authenticity is not just about you: it's also about the quality of your relationships. Getting used to making lifestyle changes like this prepares the way for doing deeper work on autopilot reactions through mindfulness meditation.

1

Appreciate kindness when people show it. Tell them that their kindness matters to you.

2

Listen to people's stories with your full attention— not just politely, but because it really matters.

Being overburdened by tasks may also be unconsciously attractive because it gives us an excuse to be selective. For example, we might have issues with a family member that we know we should address in a long heart-to-heart chat, but we fear the buried emotions such a conversation might dredge up from the past. So we tell ourselves that we just can't make time for it.

Getting to know you

Another common habitual thought pattern is a tendency to make quick judgements about people we meet, then stick to them, even though they were based on extremely flimsy evidence. In fact, giving people the chance to be who they really are, in that moment, is an attitude that follows on naturally from mindfulness.

As a counterweight to this tendency, try seeing people with fresh eyes. Ask them questions that you wouldn't normally ask; solicit their opinions; and listen attentively to what they have to say. Your perceptions will almost certainly expand beyond the blinkered view you started with. Given the limitations of our understanding, it's hardly surprising when people turn out to be nicer than we thought.

GETTING TO KNOW YOUR MIND STORMS

At times of stress, our thinking speeds up as we rush in panic from one bad thought and feeling to another, trying to find a solution. You can use these mind-storm experiences as a way into thoughtful self-analysis. Ask yourself these questions and write the answers in your mindfulness journal (see page 53):

- What kinds of situation tend to trigger your mind storms?
- Are there any thoughts that keep recurring in your mind storms? Are any of these thoughts obviously true or false?
- Are there any memories that keep coming into your mind storms? If so, why do you think they surface like this?
- Are there any recurrent emotions in your mind storm? What's the effect of such emotions on your thinking and behavior?

3

Ask a colleague their opinion about something—not a work question, but something beyond your normal range of conversational topics.

4

Talk to anyone who approaches you in the street—whether they're begging, trying to sell something, or doing a survey.

5

Don't take mobile phone calls when you're with someone: concentrate fully on being with them.

QUESTIONNAIRE: AUTHENTICITY

HOW TRUE TO YOURSELF ARE YOU?

Your true self is probably not the self of your everyday thoughts and feelings. Some deep-seated issues and emotions may be preventing your true self from expressing itself, even to its "owner." The questions here will help you examine yourself to identify the issues you're carrying and what effect they may be having upon you.

Q Do you have issues?

- How strongly do you feel there's a difference between the person you could have been, if you hadn't made mistakes, and the person you are?

- How often, after you've met new people, do you come away feeling that they were probably unimpressed by you, or didn't warm to you?

- How often, in conversation, do you feel emotions that aren't directly concerned with the subject you're talking about?

- How likely do you think it is that other people see you differently from the way you see yourself?

Q How troublesome are your issues?

- How stressed a person would you say you are, inwardly?

- How often do any anxieties show, do you think, in your body language or your tone of voice?

- How often do any anxieties have an effect on your dealings with people?

- How often do your thoughts and feelings race uncontrollably around your head while you're sitting quietly on your own?

Q Are you acting a part?

- How often do say things that you think people expect of you, rather than what you'd say otherwise?

- How often do you try to give the impression to others that you have knowledge or skills you lack?

- How often do you feign interest in a conversation, and ask questions just to keep it going?

- How strongly do you believe that different people have different ideas about what you're really like?

Q Are you dealing with your issues?

- How strongly do you believe that the answer to your problems lies within yourself rather than with others?

- How often do you share any emotional difficulties with friends, family, or your partner?

- How often do you succeed in reducing the damage caused by your issues by seeing them in their proper perspective?

- How often do you attempt to tackle your issues by creating a calmer environment for yourself?

EXPLORE FURTHER

Use this self-analysis to assess what, if any, issues are impeding the functioning of your authentic self. First, do the breathing exercise on pages 96–99 to help you ground yourself and gain some clarity. You can use mindfulness meditation to help you face these issues, get them in a truer perspective, and work through them. But even in coming to a better understanding of them, you've taken a big step forward.

CAN YOU CHANGE YOUR PRESENTED SELF?

Mindful meditation can help you find and live your true self. But first, try these straightforward ways to match the self you present to others to the private self you know.

- Start a conversation about something you really care about, and express your true opinions. See if you can end up with each of you having a clear idea of the other's views.

- Correct a false idea that someone has about you. Concentrate on the factual. If someone underestimates you, put them right tactfully and sensitively if you get the opportunity.

- Admit to ignorance rather than letting someone think you know more than you do. If you don't understand something, ask what it means.

WANDERING MIND
HOW TO CONCENTRATE BETTER

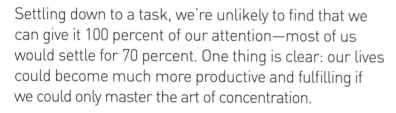

Settling down to a task, we're unlikely to find that we can give it 100 percent of our attention—most of us would settle for 70 percent. One thing is clear: our lives could become much more productive and fulfilling if we could only master the art of concentration.

Think of yourself composing an email to a friend or following a new recipe from a book in the kitchen. Do you give your wholehearted attention to the matter, or does your mind wander from time to time? Most probably, you'll confess to wandering. You might find yourself straying along a byway—a branch of thought that starts with the matter at hand but soon goes off at a tangent. Alternatively, thoughts might surface that are completely unconnected to what you're doing— perhaps reprising something you were thinking about earlier.

Worries, in particular, often resurface like this. Before starting a new task, we usually push any preoccupations to the back of our mind. But they have a nasty habit of coming back and clamoring to be noticed. Whether we give them the attention they crave depends on how mindful we can be.

Going off course

We spend a significant part of our lives engaged in "mind wandering"— daydreaming, or straying from the present moment. This can be part of the helpful process of reflecting on a problem, taking a break from it, and then returning to it later. It is important to understand that it is in the nature of the mind to wander, and this can facilitate learning.

However, mind wandering can be disruptive as well as beneficial. If unsolicited thoughts distract us from

The mind is a surreal place, where a strange thing keeps happening: the background keeps becoming the foreground.

ONE-POINTEDNESS

Meditators call concentration "one-pointedness" of mind. You keep your focus on its chosen object, with conscious effort. The other quality exercised in meditation is mindfulness, which notices when your concentration goes astray. The two should operate together. If either of these partners is performing ineffectively, the meditation works less well.

Undisciplined thoughts may flit between past, present, and future.

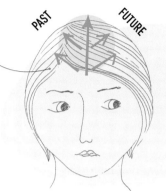

PAST   FUTURE

DISSIPATED ATTENTION
The wandering mind, during a task, misdirects energy to the mind's unconscious agenda of issues and anxieties, outside the present moment.

Focused thoughts give you clarity and a sense of achievement.

ONE-POINTED ATTENTION
The focused mind, during a task, directs its energy to single point, within the moment, and takes satisfaction from its own effectiveness.

our reading, for example, not only will we have to spend longer on the task, we might also find that we haven't absorbed much. At work or in social settings, mind wandering may affect our comprehension in meetings, making us less effective. It's been shown to make our working memory less efficient too.

But where does our mind go on its travels? Very often to our most pressing background anxieties. It's a myth to imagine that wandering thoughts are truly random, since in fact they're often following our own inner agenda.

Happy focus
Another myth is that the brain might actually enjoy its periods of idle leisure. The problem is that "leisure," or downtime, without mindfulness, can often be a place where negative thoughts and feelings thrive. This is because the brain is "hard-wired" to remember hurtful or dangerous things so that we steer clear of them in future.

A program of mindfulness meditation can reduce mind wandering, and in the process enhance our personal effectiveness as learners, communicators, and problem solvers. At the same time, by reducing the power of mental distraction, it can improve an important aspect of our general well-being.

WHAT IS FREEDOM?
Distractions don't free your thoughts—they enslave them. Only when your mind is able to focus can you truly free your thinking.

MINDFUL LEARNING

HOW TO GROW YOUR UNDERSTANDING

Being told how things are or how we must behave is something we all remember from our days at school. But learning in adult life is usually more of a process than a prescription, requiring us to be open to new ideas and willing to experiment. Mindfulness primes us to be mentally flexible for learning.

As adults, much of what we learn about life and the world outside us comes to us indirectly. For example, we might see a television program promoting the technique of interval training to improve fitness; later, on the news, we hear about a celebrity who suffered a stroke after following the practice. That prompts an internal debate about whether that form of exercise has dangers to health that outweigh its benefits. We have no way of finding out the truth directly: all we can do is carry out our own research, listen to the evidence from both sides, and reach our own, perhaps tentative conclusions. In such circumstances, there'll often be a safe option: people are generally risk averse, so the safe choice is the one most people make.

Learning from experience

In our inner lives—in our pursuit of happiness and fulfillment—we're more likely to learn from direct observations and personal experiences than from

TRADITIONAL VS. MINDFUL LEARNING

According to Harvard psychology professor Ellen J. Langer, traditional patterns of learning are restricted by deeply ingrained misconceptions—for example, that there is only one way to approach a task. Mindful learning prevents our becoming trapped in rigid thought patterns, such as how things used to be done or how other people do them. Below, we compare three facets of the traditional dogmatic learning style, with a more mindful approach to the same situation.

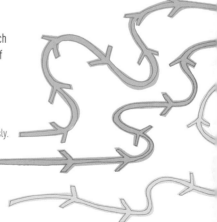

DOGMATIC LEARNING

Be focused on one thing at a time.

Memorize information by rote.

Learn the one correct answer to a question.

MINDFUL LEARNING

Create new categories continuously.

Be open to new ideas and information.

Extend your awareness to more than one perspective.

I'm an impetuous thinker. I have these impulses. What can I do to stop myself racing to conclusions?

Sit with your thoughts a little longer. Make sure when you commit to them it's intentional, not impulsive.

AVOIDING MISAPPREHENSIONS
Mindfulness gives you the space to suspend judgement and to reflect wisely on facts.

what others try to teach us. Of course, our learning does include connecting with people and sharing their experiences. As we open mindful channels of sharing, we extend our intuitive understanding of what it is, or can be, to be human.

Our learning serves us most effectively when we're adaptable to new ways of thinking, and in this respect mindfulness gives us an invaluable tool. Facing up to the truth of our experiences, however uncomfortable they are, equips us with the capacity to transform them. We learn best when we're free—from

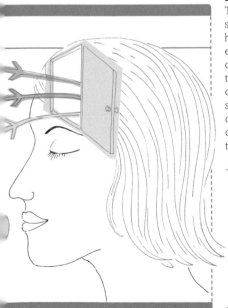

ingrained ways of thinking, from peer pressure, from worrying about what others will think, from anxieties about our intelligence or skills, and from the weight of our own expectations about ourselves.

Risk can be right
The risk-averse choice—the one that some people make when evaluating the health risks of interval training, for example—can be highly limiting in the context of our life choices. Committing to a relationship, choosing to have children, changing career, or taking a sabbatical from work all carry elements of risk. Mindfulness enables us to filter out the unhelpful and restricting fears that might cluster around a risky

decision and take a courageous path if our heart, mindfully listened to, leads us that way.

Stay flexible
The ideal of lifelong learning has shown its worth with the emergence of modern technologies. You may have no desire to become a computer geek, but if you cultivate a nimbly adaptable mindset you're unlikely to find yourself clinging to outmoded devices as if they were lifebelts in the turbulent seas of change. Charles Darwin said that it's not the strongest, nor the smartest species that survive, but the ones most adaptable to change. The lesson we learn here is that the most crucial thing you have to learn is how to learn.

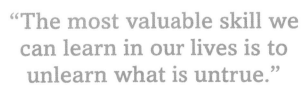

"The most valuable skill we can learn in our lives is to unlearn what is untrue."
Antisthenes (*c.*445–*c.*365BCE)

QUESTIONNAIRE: CONCENTRATION

HOW SHARP IS YOUR FOCUS?

A task that requires full concentration can fill us with foreboding, perhaps because we're reluctant to take a break from the flow of thought that we mistakenly identify as the essence of the self. The questions here will help you probe your own ability to focus, and set the scene for improvement through mindfulness practice.

Q How much of your attention do you give?

- How strongly do you feel that if you were able to concentrate more effectively, you'd get more out of life?

- How often, once you settle down to a task, do you discover you've wasted precious time by thinking about something else?

- How often do you decide, while doing a task, to interrupt it by making a phone call, making tea or coffee, or engaging in some other short break from the matter at hand?

Q How well do you listen?

- When you're trying to listen to someone with full concentration, in real life or on the radio, how often are you able to absorb more than 70 percent of the sentences spoken?

- In the same situation, how often are you able to absorb more than 80 percent of what's said?

- In the same situation, how often are you able to absorb more than 90 percent of what's said?

- How many of the main points can you normally remember of, say, a half-hour talk on the radio, five minutes after the talk is completed?

Q How closely do you read?

- When you're reading a novel, how reliably do you remember the names of characters who've appeared in the book?

- When you're reading interesting information, how often do you read with full attention, not skipping anything?

- When you're reading, how often do notice that the author has made the same point twice or written something that contradicted the information in an earlier passage?

- How often do you find yourself rereading the same paragraph, as a result of having lost track of what you've already read?

Q Do you have a healthy attitude toward tasks?

- How often does the boring nature of a task make it harder for you to concentrate?

- How often do you find that the thought of another task you have to complete makes it harder for you to finish the one you're doing?

- How much do you think that, if required, you could concentrate in a busy café as well as you could in a quiet library?

- How daunted would you be by the thought of sitting still and concentrating on something for 50 minutes?

DO YOU PRIME YOURSELF TO CONCENTRATE?

People who value the importance of good concentration, and of finishing a piece of work in a timely manner, without wasting a long time on distractions, tend to consciously prepare for their task sessions. Scan the strategies given below and ask yourself whether you apply them. If not, try some of them next time you need to study, read, write, or get some other absorbing job done at home or work.

- Do you protect yourself against interruptions—for example, by telling people you want to be left alone, putting up a do-not-disturb sign, or closing the door?

- Do you set objectives for what you want to achieve and stop work when you've achieved those objectives?

- Do you set a schedule so that you're working on the tasks that need most concentration at the optimum times of day—early in the morning when you're alert, not after a meal with alcohol, and so on?

- Do you use motivational techniques—for example, giving yourself a reward on completion, or simply imagining beforehand the satisfaction of finishing what you're setting out to do?

EXPLORE FURTHER

Think carefully about your answers to evaluate whether you're able to focus effectively on tasks or on listening, or whether your mind often wastes energy by straying off the point. If your self-analysis suggests the latter, ask yourself whether there might be a reason for this—are anxieties of some kind affecting your focus? After completing a full eight-week program of mindfulness meditations, and building mindfulness into your lifestyle, do the questionnaire again to see if your concentration has improved.

ALIVE TO OTHERS
GOOD COMMUNICATION

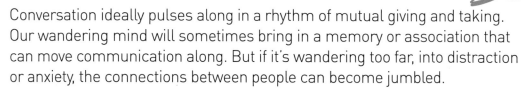

Conversation ideally pulses along in a rhythm of mutual giving and taking. Our wandering mind will sometimes bring in a memory or association that can move communication along. But if it's wandering too far, into distraction or anxiety, the connections between people can become jumbled.

A good one-to-one conversation, like a tennis match, alternates between ends. One participant switches from attending mode to speaking mode and back again, and within all this is a continuous flow of engagement. A lapse in attention on one side can cause that flow to wobble or falter by cutting off part of the connection. Anxiety in one or both of the participants can also interrupt the flow by causing an individual to direct their attention toward inner doubts rather than outward to their conversation partner.

Skill and empathy

We often speak of conversation being a skill, and in many ways it is. Certainly, it gets better with practice, because the phrases you use to join up your ideas come more readily to you. Listen to an accomplished politician being interviewed on TV or radio: their seamless weaving of words is largely down to confidence, perhaps a certain amount of training in self-presentation, but above all, practice.

However, to think of a conversation as an exercise of skill is to undervalue one of the most precious things we have—our connection with others. In a conversation that's truly alive we're giving and receiving in an exchange

QUALITY CONVERSATION

In a good conversation, you're mindfully present, attending to the relationship as well as to what's said.

Don't frame what you'll say next while you're listening to your partner: just listen, absorb, and attend to your inner reactions.

Don't make any judgements: focus on what's said, ignoring anything that isn't part of the message. Read your partner's body language, but forget about their clothes or their hairstyle.

Don't speak over them: if you feel it would be useful to interrupt, ask them if you may.

whose starting point is being together, in the moment (the "con-"in conversation, from the Latin, means "together"). If we absent ourselves from the encounter, by allowing our minds to wander, we're not truly there—so we are not conversing, only talking.

Thinking and speaking

We often choose different talking speeds and styles in different situations—from quick, spontaneous chatter over the breakfast table to slower, more deliberate conversation

when we're carefully conveying thoughts and facts. Any difficulties we might experience are likely to occur with the more measured conversations, since these are the ones about matters of importance. Talking with strangers, loose acquaintances, or people in authority can cause many types of anxiety, such as feeling ourselves inferior, at a disadvantage, nervous of how someone more "expert" might judge us, or simply not knowing what to say when we're out of our comfort zone. At the other extreme, in conversations

with close friends, family, or a partner, old patterns of blame or resentment can quickly surface and break our conversational stride.

In difficult conversations, take the time you need to decide what you want to say and then craft your language accordingly. It's important to create an opening for yourself and the person you're talking to so that your experiences and perceptions can flow. If you have lots to say, don't try to squeeze it all through too narrow a pipe, or things will get jumbled under the pressure.

> Show empathy: your conscious intent to understand others from their point of view will be felt and reciprocated.

Enjoy and be enriched: exercising your faculty of communication is natural and wholesome. Relish the encounter, enjoying its openness and discovery.

SAME PERSON: TWO CONVERSATIONS

Talking with someone while remaining fully in the present is a vital and enriching experience. But even confident, outgoing people can find themselves unable to give their attention at times. Below are two checklists of mind states. One describes someone in a conversation that goes well; the other applies to the same person on a different occasion, when for some reason they're unable to engage naturally.

MINDFUL	UNMINDFUL
Calm, relaxed.	Anxious.
Clear-minded.	Confused.
Detached from emotions.	Caught up in emotions.
Attentive.	Wandering.

POSSIBLE REASONS	
With someone liked.	With a stranger or someone disliked.
With someone pleasant to talk to.	With someone seen as challenging.
Has had a good day.	Has had a bad day.
Feeling awake.	Feeling tired.
Feeling contented.	Feeling unhappy.
Easy, enjoyable subject.	Difficult, uncomfortable subject.

QUESTIONNAIRE: CONNECTION

HOW WELL DO YOU COMMUNICATE?

Through good communication we can share and relish our common humanity, and deal with negative emotions when things go wrong. Use these questions to examine your communication style, and then employ mindfulness to help inject new energy into your relationships.

Q How well do you communicate with people close to you?

- How often do you find yourself having similar conversations over and over, making the same points, and not progressing?

- How often do your most serious conversations end in disagreement, with bad feelings on both sides?

- In your relaxed, casual conversations, how often does the other person show fresh aspects of themselves that take you by surprise?

- How much do you think that, in your conversations with these people/this person, your true self comes through, without concealment or reservation?

Q How well do you communicate with acquaintances?

- How much do you think that you tend to get to know your acquaintances better with each meeting you have with them?

- How much do you think that your acquaintances tend to get to know you better with each meeting?

- How much do you think that you tend to remember what your acquaintances told you the last two or three times you met?

- How much do you really focus, in the present moment, on your friendly chats with people you encounter by chance?

Q How well do you communicate with strangers?

- How often you do actively enjoy and feel enriched by meeting and talking to strangers?

- How much do you think that, in your conversations with strangers, your true self comes through, without concealment or holding back?

- How often when you have a conversation with a stranger do you end it thinking, "I'm free now to get on with what I was doing?"

- How often when you have a short, friendly chat with a stranger do you smile or laugh at something they say?

CAN YOU DO THE HARD STUFF?

There are challenging kinds of conversation that most people find difficult, because they involve a clash of perspectives. Success requires different characteristics in each case: sometimes you need determination or a high level of self-esteem, at other times empathy or tact. Ask yourself how well you have performed in the past across the range of situations listed below:

- Saying no to a persuasive request

- Expressing an unpopular point of view

- Asking a favor from someone who might refuse it

- Refusing a plea for help

- Explaining, clearly and calmly, how angry you are

- Responding to an insult or a sarcastic remark

- Telling a story to a large group of friends

- Putting a case to someone in authority

- Telling someone never to repeat their unacceptable behavior.

Q Can you communicate in stressful situations?

- When things are going wrong in a relationship, how often do you accept partial responsibility for the problems?

- How often do you avoid saying what you truly think, because you're afraid of the other person's reactions?

- In stressful conversations, how often do you find yourself exaggerating your feelings for effect?

- When you feel anxious or emotional in a conversation, how much do you think that these feelings impair your ability to express yourself?

EXPLORE FURTHER

Using your answers as a basis, assess whether, in different situations, you tend to be fully aware and engaged in the flow of talk, or whether in some circumstances you're more likely to become distracted rather than mindful. This isn't just a question of conversational skills: it goes right to the heart of the way you relate, in the present moment, to others. Try doing relevant parts of the questionnaire again to cover specific relationships. Mindfulness will make all your connections more open and more giving. For the moment, it's enough to know the kinds of interactions you seek to enhance.

WHO AM I?
A QUESTION OF IDENTITY

We usually don't spend much time considering the philosophical question of who we are. But there may be times when this question becomes critical, causing confusion and stress. Mindfulness enables us to find clarity by sifting personal truth from personal myth.

When you ask yourself the question, "Who am I?," there's probably no single true thought that you can hold in your mind as an answer. More likely, a variety of thoughts swarm in your head, each in turn dislodging the others as the mind's focus shines its torch restlessly over the possibilities.

Some of these thoughts will be labels attached to your roles in life (mother, father, daughter, son, friend, manager, and so on) and to your persona—the image you want to project to others. Some may be linked to your values, whether moral, political, or spiritual, and to your nationality or the local community you belong to. All these ways of describing yourself add up to a "composite" identity, which fails fully to capture the reality of who you are. Your true identity is elsewhere, impossible to pin down in words—just as you know what's meant when someone talks about the South Pole, but you don't know what it's actually like there.

You're not your public face

Anyone who wishes to know themselves more truly must give mindful attention to their public persona—the outer identity they present to the world. This is an artifice that we use for our everyday interactions with others. There are often differences between this outer self and the inner self we see as more authentic. The outer self is how we'd like to be seen—for example, as caring, efficient, smart, and so on—and it's also the ideal we try to realize. But our persona is not entirely within our control: it is partly conditioned by past experiences, so we can't always choose how we appear. When the real self finds the persona impossible to live up to, we start worrying about our true identity. Knowing how your persona operates is an important step in self-understanding. Stepping mindfully into the moment helps you see it for what it is: an artifice, not a vital aspect of your being.

"**I am a loving mother.**"
Work pressures make it hard for me to always be there for my children.

"**I'm a star, admired by all.**"
I seem to be failing more and more at work but I have to keep up the pretence of excelling at all I do.

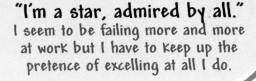

SAME AS IT NEVER WAS
The ideals of your public persona (bold type) often hide the contradictory truths that lie behind them (gray type).

IDENTITY CRISES

The composite identity we adopt helps to keep us stable in the endlessly shifting circumstances we inhabit. However, there are times when different parts of this composite identity clash, and this can trigger a crisis of confidence. Three such circumstances are described below. Practicing mindfulness lets us simply "be," giving us respite from such conflicts in times of trouble.

When our roles conflict with each other.

Our differing roles may compete for the limited time we have available, and we may feel pulled in different directions—unsure, for example, whether we're a parent or a manager. Switching repeatedly from one role to another we feel that we can't fill either role to our own or anyone else's satisfaction.

When what we privately know about ourselves parts company from the way we want people to think of us.

We may feel a pressing need to satisfy other people's expectations of our behavior, but inwardly we know we're falling short. Our public identity thus becomes a pretence.

When we start to identify with our pain.

Pain—caused by low self-esteem, a flawed relationship, or a physical or mental illness—can creep into, and become part of, our identity. Tethering ourselves to our suffering in this way has the unfortunate effect of prolonging it.

SEEING YOUR TRUE SELF
MINDFULNESS AND IDENTITY

Many people who practice mindfulness often say they feel more truly themselves during their meditations than at any other time. The experience of simply being feels authentic, clear, and calm, allowing the labels that make up the bundle of the self to be jettisoned.

Practicing mindfulness doesn't necessarily give you a clearer insight into who you are: it is more that you don't regard identity as relevant any more. This eliminates much of the confusion that can be caused by issues of self. When you step into the present moment mindfully, you're not cutting off your commitment to what you most value—for example, your loving relationship with a partner. It's simply that you aren't identifying yourself with a particular set of values. For as long as you're mindful, you're simply a person who's alive and awake in the moment, attending to present experiences. All the pressures that were impacting on your sense of the life you're living no longer exert their compelling power on your self-image: they become like light clouds, which you can see, but don't restrict your progress.

FREEDOM AND IDENTITY
When we live life mindfully, our past, future, and present concerns are perceptible but harmless—like the clouds around a balloon. As we journey through life, our values and commitments stay with us constantly but they don't define us.

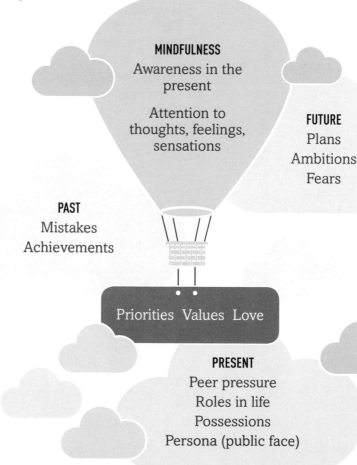

MINDFULNESS
Awareness in the present

Attention to thoughts, feelings, sensations

FUTURE
Plans
Ambitions
Fears

PAST
Mistakes
Achievements

Priorities Values Love

PRESENT
Peer pressure
Roles in life
Possessions
Persona (public face)

THE CRITIC AND THE OBSERVER

For most people, thinking is an inner monologue. There's a talker inside the mind who regales us all through the day with a running commentary on how we're doing. This person is a critic—constantly restless and dissatisfied; if we listen to him, we forget how to be content with the way life is. It is better—but often more difficult—to listen to his mind-mate, the observer, who lives in the moment and tells it like it is. Jon Kabat-Zinn has spoken of our endless swirl of thoughts and feelings as a turbulent river torrent that we get caught up in. To extend his metaphor, the critic shouts above the rushing torrent to make himself heard. The observer, meanwhile, sits calmly on the riverbank, studying the mindstream of experience. Contrast the characteristics of the critic with those of the observer in the chart below and try to identify situations when each is active in your own life.

THE CRITIC	THE OBSERVER
Enjoys the good life, preferring pleasure to pain.	Treats pain and pleasure with equanimity.
Likes to make comparisons.	Reports everything he sees.
Constantly makes judgements.	Stays within the moment.
Imitates our voice to make us listen to what he says.	Is always honest.
Exaggerates and distorts.	Has a sense of proportion.

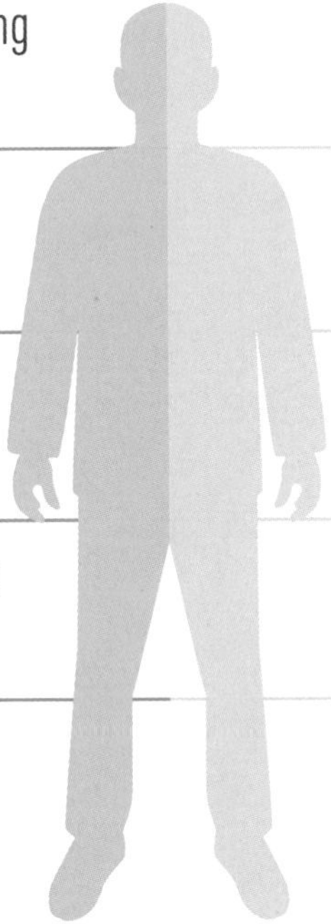

The more you listen to your inner critic, the less free your mind will be to find creative solutions to your problems.

QUESTIONNAIRE: WHAT AM I LIKE?

HOW DO YOU SEE YOURSELF?

We see ourselves in one way, but others might see us differently. If so, it may be that we've crafted an image of how we'd like to be seen, or that people see through our self-delusions. Complete this questionnaire to assess any identity issues you might have and to edge toward a clearer sense of who you are.

Q Do you identify with your roles?

- How strongly do the most important roles you play in life (as distinct from what you do in those roles) contribute to your self-esteem?

- How often do you worry that you're not just one person but two or more people, with conflicting priorities?

- How much do you think that you make personal sacrifices in order to meet people's expectations of you?

- How much do you think that your roles in life are an important part of how you want people to see you?

Q Do you identify with your achievements?

- How often do you draw personal strength from what you've achieved in your life so far?

- How strongly do you see your home, your car, or your leisure pursuits as symbols of your personal success?

- How much do you think that looking back on your past achievements helps you to be confident in company?

- How often do you take your failures deeply to heart, feeling that you've let yourself down?

REVIEW YOUR PRIORITIES

Using the pie chart here (right) as a guide, draw your own personal version with the sizes of slices reflecting which elements in your makeup you link most closely with your identity. This is not an exact science: use your intuition to draw a chart that seems approximately right.
Change the names of the concepts if you prefer different terminology or different measures.

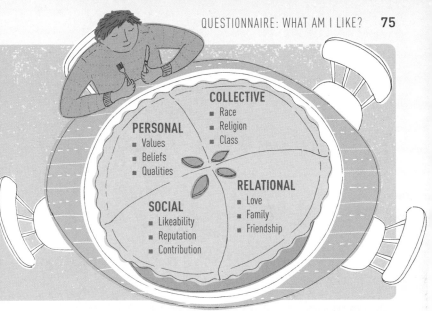

COLLECTIVE
- Race
- Religion
- Class

PERSONAL
- Values
- Beliefs
- Qualities

RELATIONAL
- Love
- Family
- Friendship

SOCIAL
- Likeability
- Reputation
- Contribution

Q Do you identify with your problems?

- How often do you feel that your problems don't allow space in your head for anything else?

- How strongly do you feel a sense that your problems are part of the landscape of your life—the place where you live?

- How strongly do you feel that it's almost impossible to imagine yourself without any problems—as someone who's happy and relaxed?

- How strongly do you feel that you've gotten used to your problems, and that to solve them would leave a vacuum in your life?

Q Do you identify with your values?

- How often, when someone challenges your values, does it feel that they're undermining you personally?

- How strongly would you like people to value you for what you believe in as much as what you do or say?

- How much do you think that anyone who doesn't understand what your values are doesn't know the real you?

EXPLORE FURTHER

Use this self-analysis to assess how you see yourself—in terms of the roles you feel you occupy, your achievements and disappointments, and your cherished beliefs. Can you trace the different components of your identity? How many of these components seem problematic to you? Consider whether—if your identity is rooted in the past—there are future directions you can take to resolve any identity issues. Resolve to use mindfulness to help you in this.

INNER CIRCLE
THE MINDFUL HOME

You can enrich your domestic life by doing chores and organizing your home mindfully. Above all, though, "home" is the people who live there, and sharing mindfulness with them is a wonderful way to open your hearts to each other.

A home is not just an empty shell. Of course it is less important than the people who live there, but it's also an environment over which we exercise our choices. Mindfulness values choices, so putting your personal stamp on your home can be an exercise of judicious choice. Mindfulness also nourishes our responsiveness, so we're likely to want an attractive environment around us—a setting for our lives to which we can respond with satisfaction. You can also view the act of enriching your home as an act of generosity—giving pleasure to others who inhabit the space.

The physical home, like a person, is vulnerable to issues: it has its ailments, its habits, and its moods. If you're living mindfully you'll take notice of these things and respond positively to them. Each remedial activity you embark on—whether washing curtains or fixing a creaky hinge—gives you the opportunity for living fully in the moment, experiencing the feel of tools and materials, absorbed in something outside your daily routine. Your home—like a garden—requires regular tending, but not so much that it interferes with getting on with your life.

Household life
In a happy household—whether you are a partner in a mindful couple, or just friends living under the same roof—the

DECLUTTERING
Decluttering your home is an ideal subject for a mindfulness exercise.

- **Discard**: pick up and examine items in turn and attend to your thoughts. How would you feel about discarding an item? You might have feelings about losing a connection with the past. Attend to such feelings without judgment. Remind yourself that you're living in the present: the past can be an encumbrance, with a tendency to drain your energy if you allow it too much power.

- **Tidy**: clutter is distracting, reminding you each time you see it that there's a job to be done. Be decisive and tidy mindfully, observing your own reactions as the room starts to acquire more order. Do you feel satisfaction as you clear the detritus of the past?

> "A house is not a home unless it contains food and fire for the mind as well as the body."
> Benjamin Franklin

sense of being on a mindful adventure together can bring excitement both to the discoveries you make and to the relationship itself.

Children add to the pleasure, not least because they have not yet had time to get set in their ways. Sharing mindfulness with them, and hearing them talk in a mindful way, extends your empathic connection with them and provides a foundation for their growth into maturity.

You can extend mindful living into your home life in many ways. The simplest is to appreciate what you have, rather than taking possessions for granted. Think about what it takes to create, make, and bring an object to you. How many people has this involved? Who and where might they be? In the same spirit, consider new purchases carefully—mindfully deciding not to buy something is an alternative, and very satisfying, form of retail therapy.

THREE MINDFUL CHORES

Use household chores as simple mindfulness practices. Gently attend to your chosen object of focus in the moment, avoiding any judgment about yourself or your feelings. Approach the chores in a positive spirit. If resentment creeps it, observe it with curiosity: don't get absorbed in it.

SWEEP LEAVES IN THE GARDEN

This is a classic Zen Buddhist mindfulness practice. Attend in turn to the moving leaves, the rhythm of your body's efforts, your breathing, and the rustling sounds. Let all other sensations go, as well as any thoughts or feelings.

MAKE YOUR BED WITH FULL AWARENESS

Attend to the sensations in your body as you move. Each time you become aware of a thought or feeling, or an extraneous sound in the home, return your attention gently to bedmaking.

DO YOUR LAUNDRY MINDFULLY

Relish the feel of the fabrics and the way they fold into each other. Be aware of the mechanical sound and movements of the washing machine as it starts. Watch and listen to it for a minute or so, letting go of all other thoughts, sensations, and feelings.

WITHIN YOUR GRASP

GETTING REAL ABOUT YOUR HAPPINESS

If our ideal of happiness is borrowed from a daydream of living a different life, we're unlikely to attain it. And pursuing happiness too earnestly can push it further away from us. Better to reevaluate what happiness means to us: we may well find that we had it all along.

Assessing, from time to time, whether you've attained the happiness you've been looking for is far from straightforward. It involves making a judgement about your experiences by measuring them against a preference. What if you apply your yardstick and discover that you fall short of being happy? Until now, you didn't know that. In this scenario, is checking for happiness—and nothing else—the very thing that makes you *un*happy?

Measurement of joy

First, there's the question of how you measure your happiness. The yardstick most people employ is some kind of mental comparison that rates your happiness level not against your own previous level, nor someone else's level,

IS HAPPINESS WHAT WE THINK IT IS?

Could it be that the most precious form of happiness is very different from what you've been conditioned to aspire to? Here are some ideas you may not be familiar with:

TRUE HAPPINESS IS

- The bliss we find when we enter the moment

- A serenity that underlies and permeates all emotional states, including sorrow

- Our state of mind when what we say, do, and think are in all in harmony

- Moving forward wholeheartedly without reservation or regret

- The consequence that flows from good-hearted intentions.

> We create the image of a happy life from fragments of an imaginative story we weave around ourselves.

but against an ideal—a level that you would consider to be satisfactory… that makes you happy. The problem with such ideals is that life's too complicated for them to be of much use. We create the image of a happy life from fragments of an imaginative story we weave around ourselves.

Missing the point

Our aspirations to happiness can block our true perceptions, preventing us from seeing our life in the richness it already possesses. Reaching for our happiness yardstick, we miss experiences that could be of great value to us—indeed, we resist them, imagining that they need to be altered, and not realizing that they contain life-changing insights. Moreover, we also miss out on the happiness that lies at the heart of the moment, in the appreciation of life's beauty and wonder.

HAPPINESS AND MINDFULNESS TOGETHER?

Mindfulness brings us the following gifts, which make us happy. Happiness enriches those gifts, which make us happier still. Being mindful also blocks routes to unhappiness: it stops us regretting, pondering, and living in a state of anxiety about future events.

Enhanced relationships

Clearer thinking

A more positive outlook

Better health

More creativity

A HAPPY PRACTICE
Living in expectation of gifts brings only frustration; treating each moment as a gift is a mindful way to happiness.

"To the mind that is still, the whole universe surrenders."

Lao Tzu (*c*.694–*c*.531BCE)

THE BIGGER PICTURE
TOWARD THE MEANING OF LIFE

Happiness and meaning are both nebulous ideas. It's no surprise that many people are troubled by them, unsure if they're present in their lives, at least potentially, and if so, how to find them. Mindfulness, as always, provides a roadmap—and helps to set the compass too.

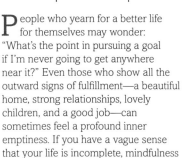

People who yearn for a better life for themselves may wonder: "What's the point in pursuing a goal if I'm never going to get anywhere near it?" Even those who show all the outward signs of fulfillment—a beautiful home, strong relationships, lovely children, and a good job—can sometimes feel a profound inner emptiness. If you have a vague sense that your life is incomplete, mindfulness can help you find wholeness.

Is happiness enough?
It's easy when thinking about happiness to fall into a trap that's largely a matter of words. You believe that you're happy, but in the background of your thoughts there is a distant hum of unease when you start reflecting on the question. You guess that might be because your life lacks meaning: you don't understand how you fit into the scheme of things, and you're worried about losing what you have—as inevitably you one day will. When the good things fade away, what will you have to replace them?

It's this kind of thinking that often leads people on a spiritual quest: they find purpose in religion, with its rituals

and sacred texts, or in a more freestyle version of spirituality. Such explorations can lead to deep truths, but they're not for everyone.

Concepts and realities
We form our concept of happiness by making a generalization about particulars—so, for example, you believe you are happy because you have a loving spouse, a good income, sound health, and so on. In the process of generalizing, you take a step back from reality—from the moment.

Mindfulness is a term applied to conscious awareness of present experience, without judgment. By extension, it encourages us not to become too attached to the concept of happiness.

Beyond happiness
If you feel unease in your life, mindfulness practice will invite you into an intimate relationship with that feeling. As you attend to your unease, the idea of happiness falls away. And so does the question that's been

> If you're moving to become an authentic human being, and the best version of yourself that's possible, then your life has as much meaning as anyone could hope for.

bothering you: namely, is your problem that you lack higher purpose, or is it more that you're not as happy as you thought you were? That too is irrelevant to present experience. It's only words, and your unease lies beyond words. In fact, words can sometimes make your disquiet worse by bringing a sense of intellectual confusion into the mix. Mindfulness allows you to be with yourself, not trapped in some notion of how you should be based on your external circumstances. It makes space for authentic happiness to emerge.

The question, "What is the meaning of my life?," dissolves into oblivion once, through mindfulness meditation, you discover you can be at peace in your mind, in the moment. Given time and practice, acceptance, empathy, and compassion flow from this still point of the self. You start to understand that humanity's sufferings are caused by people being unable to access an inner source of nourishment that's potentially available to all. And when you yourself are struggling to cope, that's because you're looking at your life from an unhelpful perspective. From the true, mindful perspective, life has its own meaning, which spreads to encompass those to whom you bring your precious gifts. We practice mindfulness not to become something special but because we already are something special.

THE GOLDEN PILLAR

The qualities and values that give our existence true meaning have been compared to a golden pillar—a pure, incorruptible support for a virtuous and satisfying life. Many people, however, build their lives around false meanings, which—though perhaps temporarily attractive—are ultimately no more than fool's gold. Others still adopt values that may be worthwhile, but fall short of the absolute. Mindfulness meditation makes the golden pillar accessible, in its sanctum of the awakened self.

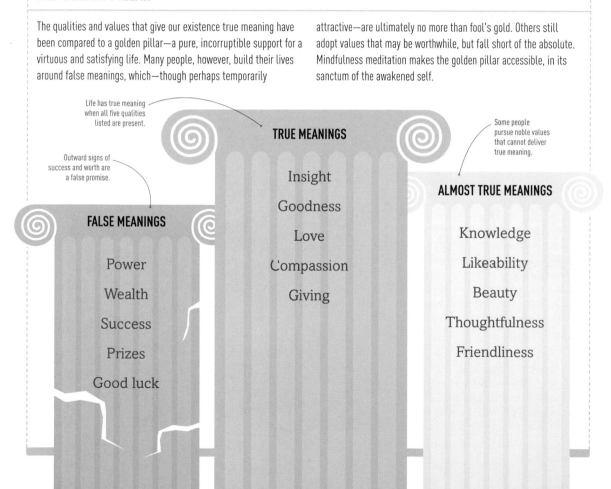

Life has true meaning when all five qualities listed are present.

Outward signs of success and worth are a false promise.

Some people pursue noble values that cannot deliver true meaning.

TRUE MEANINGS

Insight
Goodness
Love
Compassion
Giving

FALSE MEANINGS

Power
Wealth
Success
Prizes
Good luck

ALMOST TRUE MEANINGS

Knowledge
Likeability
Beauty
Thoughtfulness
Friendliness

MINDFULNESS MEDITATION

THE KEY MEDITATIONS OF MINDFULNESS, FROM FOCUSING ON AN OBJECT TO WORKING WITH BODY AND BREATH, WILL OPEN THE DOOR TO A HAPPIER LIFE.

GETTING STARTED
INTRODUCING MEDITATION PRACTICE

In this chapter, you'll be introduced to the core mindfulness meditation practices. You'll learn that they are not strange, esoteric rituals but can be readily integrated into your everyday life. Your mindfulness journey starts here.

When you meditate, it's as if your sensations, thoughts, and feelings are in an aquarium, behind a glass wall. You pull up a chair and sit there calmly watching them. It's peaceful in the aquarium—though in the tank itself, where all kinds of dramas play themselves out, it can be rather chaotic.

Now, more than ever, you become the observer (see page 73); you don't invite your inner critic along, since mindfulness means being purposefully in the moment without judgement. If you notice that he's crept in, just ignore him: he'll soon go away if you pay him no attention.

Formal meditation practice simply involves setting aside time for a meditation session at some point in your day, every day. You can choose how long, but five or ten minutes is a good starting point if you are a complete novice.

An everyday practice

You may have heard myths about meditation (see box, right), but be assured that there's no ritual involved: you don't need to wear special clothes, have a talisman nearby, fill the room with mood music, or burn incense. You simply decide when you're going

FIVE MEDITATION TIPS FOR BEGINNERS

When you begin your practice, meditation will be unfamiliar and you might feel a little lost. Keep in mind these five very simple tips—they'll help you find your way. Write them into your meditation journal, and review them before each session, making your own notes about which tips are useful—and which not.

1

Have warm feelings toward yourself—what many meditators call "self-compassion." Be generous and caring.

2

Prepare yourself to observe and learn: that's the only intention you should take into your meditation.

> My mindfulness meditation didn't work. I couldn't stop myself worrying.

> You have learned something about yourself. Have patience and persist.

NO MAGIC BULLET
While some people gain tangible benefits from practice in just a few weeks, it's not the same for everyone.

to meditate, and do it—for a predetermined period. Ideally, you should meditate daily, but aim to practice at least every other day if you can't manage that level of commitment. You can choose from a wide variety of core practices, such as meditating on your breath, body, objects, or feelings, all of which are described in detail on the following pages. You could practice each one for a couple of weeks before moving on to the next, and in this way choose what suits you best. Alternatively, you could combine different meditations into a program for variety (see pages 88–91). The choice is yours—there's no right or wrong way.

TEN MYTHS ABOUT MEDITATION
The practice of meditation is much misunderstood. Here are some common myths:

1   Meditation is a technique for relaxing
2   Meditation requires a serene haven or temple
3   When meditating you concentrate hard
4   When meditating you empty your mind
5   Meditators are always highly spiritual people
6   Meditators must sit on the floor, legs crossed
7   You need a calm mind to meditate
8   Meditation is a form of self-hypnosis
9   Meditators control their own thoughts
10 Meditations either work or fail.

3
Forgive your own lapses: if you don't practice when you meant to, don't feel bad about it. Nothing is lost: just invite yourself back into the present moment.

4
Find a mindfulness pal: having someone to share your meditation experiences with isn't essential, but may help to boost your motivation and commitment.

5
Thank yourself afterward—show gratitude to yourself for caring enough to meditate mindfully in your busy life.

MIXING AND MATCHING

PLANNING YOUR PRACTICE

When you begin your mindfulness practice, you might worry if you're doing it right: are you doing the right meditations in the right order for the right length of time? Such anxiety is unnecessary: mindfulness is a principle, and there's infinite room for variation in the way that principle is applied.

There's no set prescription for doing successful mindfulness practice. Some people like to focus on one or more of the core mindfulness meditations described in this chapter (and listed in the box, right); others like to mix and match their meditations to suit their own preferences, while others still prefer to embark on and follow a more methodical program.

The pioneers of modern mindfulness, such as Jon Kabat-Zinn, initially devised an eight-week program, based on their experience of working with a range of people in a therapeutic setting. However, there's nothing magical about this eight week span—it's simply a long enough period of time for the benefits of mindfulness meditation to have a good chance of showing; and it offers a sufficiently

How long should I meditate for?

When you begin, aim for 10-15 minutes per day. You'll most likely find it hard to focus for longer at first. Aim to gradually increase the time to 20-30 minutes to gain greater benefits from your practice.

TIME FOR YOU
Some meditation every day is better than none: don't berate yourself if you can afford only a few minutes.

large framework for a buildup of practice, with plenty of variety to help to motivate the beginner.

Programs for progress

On pages 90–91 you'll find three programs of differing lengths for you to try if you wish. The structures offered are intended to be helpful rather than prescriptive. Once you've committed to one of the program≤s, and perhaps adapted it to fit the regular routines of your life, you will no longer have to make decisions about how to make mindfulness work for you: you simply do it, following the recipe given. However, if one day you can't find the time, or feel like giving mindfulness a break, you can do so without feeling guilt or anxiety. Feel free to devise your own schedule in the light of your time commitments and the experiences you have during practice.

Meditation times

Just as with your choice of meditation practice, there's no right or wrong answer when deciding how long or how regularly to meditate. In one study, where people had trained in meditation for eight weeks, the average duration of a session at the end of the course was 23 minutes a day. Participants showed much higher activation of those brain areas associated with well-being and lower activation of the areas linked with stress. While a daily meditation lasting 20 minutes or so has been proven to be effective, some people report that their stress reduces and their happiness increases with just ten minutes of mindfulness meditation daily.

Moving on

After completing your first program, you'll know enough about mindfulness in practice to be able to make your own decision about the way forward. You might choose, for example, to do a complete program repeatedly, punctuating this with interludes of less frequent meditation. If you feel unable to craft your own routine, but feel that you're gaining from what you've done so far, just continue—with any modifications you need to make for practical reasons.

FORMAL PRACTICES

This book contains step-by-step descriptions of the following mindfulness meditations:

BREATHING PRACTICE: PAGES 96–99
BODY-AND-BREATH PRACTICE: PAGES 106–109
OBJECT PRACTICE: PAGES 114–19
BODY SCAN: PAGES 120–25
WALKING MEDITATION: PAGES 132–35
LOVING KINDNESS MEDITATION: PAGES 139–41
MOUNTAIN MEDITATION: PAGES 144–47

You can also meditate in less formal settings: some other possible meditations are described on the following pages:

SWEEPING LEAVES: PAGES 22–23
HOUSEHOLD CHORES: PAGES 76–77

The breath and body-and-breath practices are fundamental meditations, so you're advised to become comfortable with these before progressing. Later, you are likely to be drawn to some practices more than to others: if you're an instinctively compassionate person, for example, the loving kindness meditation is likely to appeal. And if you love nature and the outdoors, practicing the mountain meditation may feel most natural.

In the deeper practices, such as the body scan, you may find yourself confronting uncomfortable emotions. If so, don't push yourself: pull back if it's too upsetting. Return to the simpler breath and body-and-breath practices for a while. Build up again slowly to the deeper meditations if and when you feel ready.

MINDFULNESS MEDITATIONS
THREE WEEK-BY-WEEK PROGRAMS

Following a program of meditation brings structure to your mindfulness work. Like a calendar, it exists to serve, not to restrict you. Here are three programs for those who prefer some guidance in their explorations.

These pages offer a specially devised eight-week program, alongside two shorter programs, for those who would like to sample a structured course. You can shorten or extend any of these programs to suit your needs or inclinations. The hope is that after completing one of the courses, you'll feel confident enough to build elements of it into your everyday life indefinitely from now on.

1 BEGINNER'S BREATH AND BODY

FOUR WEEKS
10 MINUTES PER DAY, BUILDING UP TO 30 MINUTES PER DAY

week 1 **Breathing practice** 10 minutes per day.
Apply mindfulness to at least two meals, two household chores, and two half-hour walks.

week 2 **Breathing practice** 20 minutes per day.
Try **walking meditation** as well, and apply mindfulness to at least two meals, two household chores, and two half-hour walks.

week 3 **Body-and-breath practice** 20 minutes every other day, alternated with **walking meditation** or **breathing practice**.
Try **object practice** as well, continue with mindful meals, chores, and walks as you wish, and try mindful conversations too.

week 4 **Body-and-breath practice** 30 minutes every day, with **walking meditation** or **breathing, object, or mountain practice** whenever you feel like it, instead or in addition. Continue your informal mindfulness in activities and conversations.

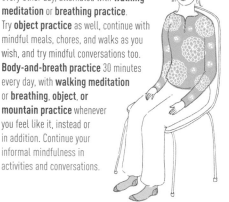

2 BEGINNER'S BREATH, BODY, AND INSIGHT

SIX WEEKS
10 MINUTES PER DAY, BUILDING UP TO 30 MINUTES PER DAY

week 1 **Breathing practice** 10 minutes per day.
Apply mindfulness to at least two meals, two household chores, and two half-hour walks.

week 2 **Breathing practice** 20 minutes per day.
Try **walking meditation** as well, and apply mindfulness to at least two meals, two household chores, and two half-hour walks.

week 3 **Body-and-breath practice** 20 minutes every other day, alternated with **walking meditation** or **breathing practice**.
Try **object practice** as well, continue with mindful meals, chores, and walks as you wish, and try mindful conversations too.

week 4 **Body scan** 30 minutes every day, with **walking meditation** or **breathing**, **object**, or **mountain practice** whenever you feel like it, instead or in addition.
Continue your informal mindfulness in activities and conversations.

week 5 **Body scan** 30 minutes every day, with **walking meditation** or **breathing**, **object**, or **mountain practice** whenever you feel like it, instead or in addition.
Continue your informal mindfulness in activities and conversations.

week 6 **Body scan** 30 minutes every day, with **walking meditation** or **breathing**, **object**, or **mountain practice** whenever you feel like it, instead or in addition.
Try **loving kindness meditation** as well, instead of one of the body scans. Continue your informal mindfulness in activities and conversations.

3 FULL BREATH, BODY, AND INSIGHT

EIGHT WEEKS
10 TO 30 MINUTES PER DAY, BUILDING UP TO 40 MINUTES PER DAY IF YOU WISH

week 1 **Breathing practice** 10 minutes per day.
Apply mindfulness to at least two meals, two household chores, and two half-hour walks.

week 2 **Body-and-breath practice** 20 minutes every other day, alternated with **walking meditation** or **breathing practice**.
And apply mindfulness to at least two meals, two household chores, and two half-hour walks.

week 3 **Body-and-breath practice** 20 minutes every other day, alternated with **walking meditation** or **breathing practice**.
Try **object practice** as well, continue with mindful meals, chores, and walks, and try mindful conversations too.

week 4 **Body-and-breath practice** 20 minutes every other day, alternated with **walking meditation** or **breathing practice**.
Try **object practice** as well, and continue with mindful meals, chores, walks, and conversations.

week 5 **Body scan** 30 minutes every day, with **walking meditation** or **breathing**, **object**, or **mountain practice** whenever you feel like it, instead or in addition.
Continue your informal mindfulness practices.

week 6 **Body scan** 30 to 40 minutes every day, with **walking meditation** or **breathing**, **object**, or **mountain practice** instead whenever you feel like it.
Continue your informal mindfulness practices.

week 7 **Body scan** 30 to 40 minutes every day, with **walking meditation** or **breathing**, **object**, or **mountain practice** instead if you wish—but do at least four body scans.
Also, do at least two **loving kindness practices**.
Continue your informal mindfulness practices.

week 8 **Body scan** 30 to 40 minutes every other day, alternating with **loving kindness practice**; do **walking meditation** or **breathing**, **object**, or **mountain practice** instead on one or two days if you wish—but do at least three body scans and two **loving kindness practices**.

GENTLY DOES IT
MEDITATION BASICS

Mindfulness meditation is easy and not at all daunting. It involves sitting in a quiet room and following a few simple guidelines. Whatever experiences you have during your meditation will be valuable to you when you reflect on them afterward.

A common error made by people who've never meditated before is to enter into it with determination and with a definite aim in mind. In many aspects of life, setting goals—and measuring your progress—is desirable.

It's what propels you forward in your career or other areas of ambition. Meditation is different: holding in mind a goal—a concept of where your meditation will lead—will interfere with the actual experience. Mindfulness is

not goal-driven and reaching a state of true awareness involves complete openness, rather than fixed purpose. Mindfulness meditation is the practice of awareness—in the moment, purposefully, and without judgement.

ATTENTION AND EXPERIENCE

Being in a mindful state is a novel but liberating experience for most people. When practicing mindfulness meditation, you:

- Direct your attention
- Sustain your attention
- Are open to experience
- Accept experience
- Let go of experience.

ALLOWING SPACE FOR THOUGHTS

Your first mindfulness meditation will involve focusing on your breathing. As you do this, fully attending to what it feels like as each breath passes through your body, you'll have a clear focus. When you wish to let go of any stray thoughts that enter your mind, you'll have an easy way to do it—gently refocus your attention on your breath. If in addition to conscious breathing you mentally counted your breaths, there would be less space in your mind for those stray thoughts. But mindfulness meditations don't involve counting, because leaving space in your mind for stray thoughts is a good thing: you observe those thoughts and let them go.

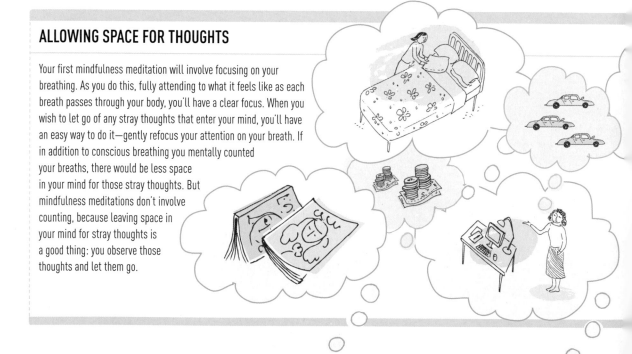

Holding in mind a goal—a concept of where your meditation will lead—will interfere with the actual meditation experience.

The exercises that you're about to embark upon are in essence very easy—so much so that "exercise" is not quite the right word, since it implies effort and technique. The only effort you apply is the decision to start and continue, until the time comes to stop; during the meditation, you apply your mind lightly and purposefully to your chosen focus. There are no techniques to learn. If you start to think you're doing it wrong, that's a judgement about yourself—and the point of mindfulness is to suspend judgement altogether. If you worry that your mind is constantly being pulled away from your meditation, that too is a sort of judgement. In fact, your mind is always going to be pulled away from its focus by all sorts of things—memories, sensations, feelings, speculations— and that's what you can expect to happen when you meditate. It's from that process that you learn important truths: the noticing of distraction and return to focus *is* the practice.

The mindful way to deal with distracting thoughts, feelings, and sensations in a meditation is to be aware of them and then let them go. Awareness is the whole point of the meditation, and opens the door to self-understanding. Letting go is not getting drawn into any of the things that pop into your mind unbidden, not engaging in any kind of dialogue with them. You're the observer, not the critic, and the observer just observes.

SWEEPING THOUGHTS AWAY

If you find the idea of letting go of thoughts tricky to grasp, here's a metaphor that may help. Imagine you're in your garden, and it's snowing. As the flakes fall and settle, you sweep them gently away with a broom. For as long as it's snowing, you have to keep sweeping to keep the garden clear. Your sweeping is not a fight with the snowflakes, just an act of clearance. You aren't controlling them or denying them— in fact, you're acknowledging them. But you're detached and relaxed about their existence, while not letting them gain a hold.

Focus on your breathing. Notice the stray thoughts that pass across your mind. Let them go.

BODY READY
SITTING WITH AWARENESS

Sitting while meditating allows you to be upright and alert, while remaining relaxed: most beginners prefer to sit on a chair rather than on the floor. Remember that this isn't exercise—the key thing is what you do with your mind, not what you do with your feet or legs.

Before you begin meditation practice, try this experiment to introduce you to the types of sensations you will feel. Move your focus around your body. Do you notice any of the following?

- **Sitting**
  Pressure from the floor and chair on your feet and legs
- **Tension in some muscles**
  The tension changes as you breathe
- **Movement in chest, rib cage, abdomen**
  The sound and feel of air moving
- **Effect of emotions and mood**
  Sensations of frowning, yawning
- **Physical needs**
  Fatigue, hunger, thirst

While your mind constantly flits to and fro, visiting the past and the future, your body is always reliably in the present. So it is no surprise that the most reliable way to begin your mindfulness practice is to tune in to the sensations of your own body.

Your body is perpetually inviting you to the here and now: accepting this invitation is the basis for your first mindfulness meditation—and will become a familiar home to return to in all your future practices. Most people opt to start their meditation practice in a sitting position because it is familiar, comfortable, accessible almost anywhere, and helps you remain alert yet relaxed.

Getting set

To begin, dress in loose clothes—or loosen any tight belts or cuffs—and find a quiet place where you won't be disturbed. Sit in an upright chair (see page 98) or cross-legged on a cushion on the floor. Follow the guidelines given here to find a posture that is comfortable and doesn't require effort to maintain. Think of yourself as a mountain: stable, balanced, grounded, dignified.

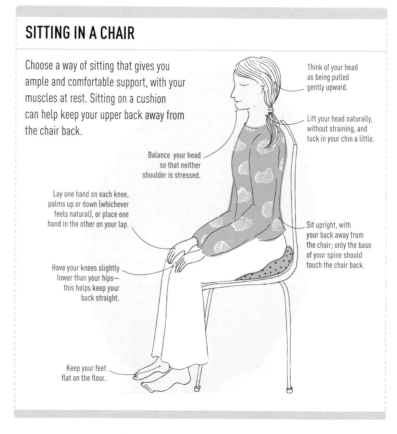

SITTING IN A CHAIR

Choose a way of sitting that gives you ample and comfortable support, with your muscles at rest. Sitting on a cushion can help keep your upper back away from the chair back.

Think of your head as being pulled gently upward.

Lift your head naturally, without straining, and tuck in your chin a little.

Balance your head so that neither shoulder is stressed.

Lay one hand on each knee, palms up or down (whichever feels natural), or place one hand in the other on your lap.

Sit upright, with your back away from the chair; only the base of your spine should touch the chair back.

Have your knees slightly lower than your hips—this helps keep your back straight.

Keep your feet flat on the floor.

SITTING ON THE FLOOR

If you are supple, for example if you have practiced yoga, you may prefer to sit on the floor rather than on a chair, raising your buttocks on a cushion. Here are three popular meditation postures.

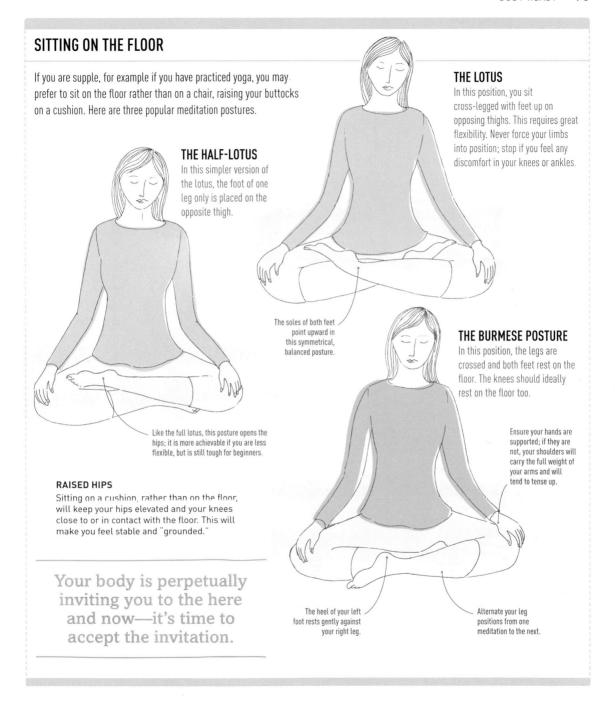

THE LOTUS
In this position, you sit cross-legged with feet up on opposing thighs. This requires great flexibility. Never force your limbs into position; stop if you feel any discomfort in your knees or ankles.

THE HALF-LOTUS
In this simpler version of the lotus, the foot of one leg only is placed on the opposite thigh.

The soles of both feet point upward in this symmetrical, balanced posture.

THE BURMESE POSTURE
In this position, the legs are crossed and both feet rest on the floor. The knees should ideally rest on the floor too.

Ensure your hands are supported; if they are not, your shoulders will carry the full weight of your arms and will tend to tense up.

Like the full lotus, this posture opens the hips; it is more achievable if you are less flexible, but is still tough for beginners.

RAISED HIPS
Sitting on a cushion, rather than on the floor, will keep your hips elevated and your knees close to or in contact with the floor. This will make you feel stable and "grounded."

Your body is perpetually inviting you to the here and now—it's time to accept the invitation.

The heel of your left foot rests gently against your right leg.

Alternate your leg positions from one meditation to the next.

BREATHE EASY
STEP-BY-STEP MINDFUL BREATHING PRACTICE

We're always breathing, though usually we're unaware of it. In this meditation you bring your attention to your breaths, while noticing any distractions and letting them go. It's the nature of the mind to wander, so you'll need to make space for and acknowledge these distractions.

Whenever you breathe differently from usual (for example, when you're walking up a steep hill or experiencing a strong emotion), you might consciously become aware of and register your breathing. But at other times, you are oblivious to the process—your mind is on other things.

The continuity of our breathing makes it an ideal subject for a mindfulness meditation. It gives us a permanently available way to anchor ourselves in the present moment.

Relax: just do it

Don't worry at all about how long you spend on your meditation. The first time you try it, five minutes will probably feel like a long time to be in "being" mode, as it's profoundly different from your normal "doing" state. You might find yourself getting mentally restless, wondering whether your meditation is working, whether you're going to be able to persist with it, or whether you're a suitable subject. It's completely normal for your mind to wander like this and it would be extraordinary if—so early in your meditation practice—your focus remained on your breathing. Don't be discouraged—keep at it. And remember Jon Kabat-Zinn's advice to beginners: you don't have to enjoy your meditation. Just commit to it, and the benefits will unfold in due course.

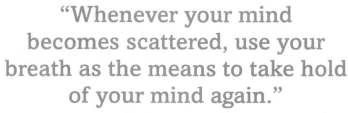

"Whenever your mind becomes scattered, use your breath as the means to take hold of your mind again."

Thích Nhat Hanh

WHAT YOU NOTICE WHEN YOU BREATHE

We breathe all day long—and when we are asleep—without it reaching conscious awareness. When we make our breathing the focus of a mindful meditation, it's not a question of thinking of "taking" breaths in and out, but of "noticing" our breath as it arrives and departs. This distinction is more than just semantics—it underlies the practice of mindfulness meditation where we don't identify with things that arise in the field of awareness, we just experience them. When you breathe, you're likely to experience the sensation in a number of ways—a passage of air, muscular movement, pressure, or a tickle in your nose (see below). Choose the one you want to focus on, and direct your attention there during this meditation.

Cool air entering the nostrils on the in-breath, warmer air leaving on the out-breath.

Rib cage rising and falling within your chest.

Movement of the belly outward as the breath arrives, inward as the breath exits.

DEALING WITH DISTRACTION AND DISCOMFORT

When the mind wanders, don't worry. There's no need for you to criticize yourself: just gently bring your attention back to your breathing. It's mindful in itself to notice when your mind is wandering and then to do something about it—realigning your mind with your breathing can give you a real sense of accomplishment.

It's not just thoughts and emotions that can distract you in a mindfulness meditation: physical discomfort can arise from your posture as aches or tensions affect your knees or your back. If this happens, you have two options:

IF THE DISCOMFORT IS TRIVIAL
Remain seated as you are, but be aware of the physical sensations you're having—their location and their intensity. Be aware too of your habitual tendency to quickly label things as either pleasant, unpleasant, or neutral—experiment with bringing a "beginner's mind" to your sensations. Accept them with friendly curiosity. It's possible that these sensations will change as you sit there.

IF THE DISCOMFORT IS GREATER
Adjust your sitting position with mindfulness. Don't just react, by shifting immediately. Instead, make your movement slowly, incorporating it into your mindful meditation, with nonjudgemental awareness.

continued ▶

FIVE-MINUTE MINDFUL BREATHING MEDITATION

This exercise, one of the cornerstones of mindfulness practice, makes a good starting point for a beginner, and an ideal basis for the first week of a mindfulness meditation program.

1 Choose a comfortable upright chair rather than an armchair or recliner. Adjustable chairs are ideal: set the height so that your feet are flat on the floor, and tilt the seat a little forward so the base of your spine just touches the chair back.

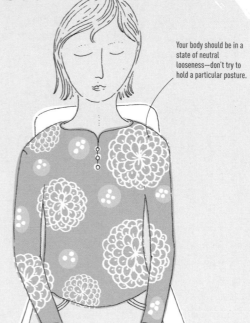

Your body should be in a state of neutral looseness—don't try to hold a particular posture.

Support your hands on your thighs, palms down.

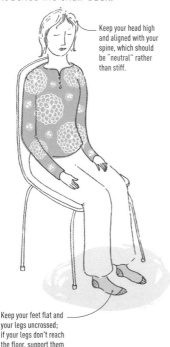

Keep your head high and aligned with your spine, which should be "neutral" rather than stiff.

Keep your feet flat and your legs uncrossed; if your legs don't reach the floor, support them on a folded blanket.

2 Close your eyes or, if you prefer, lower your gaze so it falls, unfocused, on the floor a few feet from your feet. Rest your hands on your thighs—whether they are touching or not doesn't matter.

3 Allow your body to relax and let your mind become calm. At the same time, stay alert and aware. If you find you can't relax the first few times you try it, and this instruction is just making it harder to do so, just move on to step 4.

4 Now attend to your breath. Focus on the sensations of each in-breath and out-breath wherever they are most noticeable. Some people find it best to focus on the rise and fall of their belly—the lower abdomen—but others choose to focus instead on the air entering and leaving the nose.

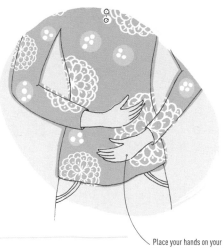

Place your hands on your belly if you wish; this may help you attend to its movements as you breathe in and out.

"When you are breathing and know that you are breathing, that is mindfulness of breathing."

Soren Gordhamer

ABOUT THE PRACTICE

Benefits A core mindfulness practice. A constantly available way to connect with the present moment. A good introduction to mindfulness meditation.

Frequency Do this every day for the first week of regular practice. After this week, progress to the body-and-breath meditation, which is an extension of this meditation (see pages 106–109).

Duration Start with a five-minute meditation, then extend the practice up to ten minutes when you feel ready.

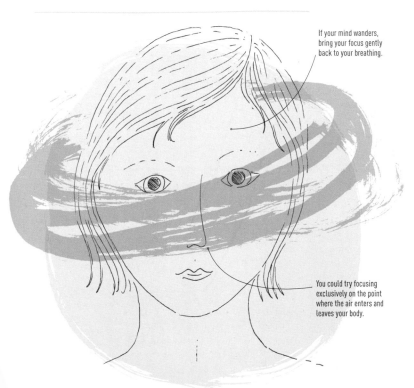

If your mind wanders, bring your focus gently back to your breathing.

You could try focusing exclusively on the point where the air enters and leaves your body.

5 Allow your breath to breathe itself as it does every moment of your life—don't try to breathe especially deeply. All you're doing now is focusing your mind on something you'd normally take for granted—a natural process that has been a part of your experience since the first moments of your life.

6 After about five minutes of mindful breathing, open your eyes and take in your surroundings again. Some people prefer to set a timer to measure out their session, while others find this distracting, because they anticipate its alarm. Do what you prefer.

INNER CLOUDS
LETTING GO OF THOUGHTS

It's possible to see thoughts passing through our minds like clouds flitting across the sky. When you do a mindfulness meditation, you notice these thoughts, and attend to the experience of having them, but you don't empower them by exerting any mental energy on them.

Mindfulness meditation involves the purposeful directing of your attention, and that includes observing your thoughts as they pass across your mind. These thoughts will often exert a strong gravitational force, whose natural tendency is to pull you into their underlying narrative.

From time to time as you meditate, you'll suddenly be aware of having left your chosen focus of attention. You'll be in a thought instead. Having noticed you're in a thought, you'll already have detached yourself from it: you must have done so momentarily, or you wouldn't have noticed. Waking up from being lost in thought is a moment for which you can congratulate yourself. These moments of "waking up" enable you to see the thought for what it is—a visitor, knocking on your door when you're busy meditating. It's noteworthy that you've had this thought, even though you don't want to accept its invitation to carry on thinking it.

Light and dark clouds

Some thoughts pass lightly through your mind like little wispy clouds. A casual remark someone made to you ten minutes ago, for example, might send a light echo through your head. Other thoughts are tangled up with

YOU ARE NOT YOUR THOUGHTS

Many of our thoughts, and especially our most troubled ones, have a personal quality to them: they feel like "me." One of the things that's most likely to undermine our self-esteem is to identify with negative thoughts like those below.

By separating yourself from such me-statements as they pass through your mind, and observing them without judgement, you see them for what they are: thoughts, not facts. As you repeat this process throughout your mindfulness meditation program, their compelling hold over you will weaken. You are you not your thoughts about yourself.

I'm not good with people.

I don't have anything interesting to say.

I'm not one of life's winners.

BREAKING FREE FROM A THOUGHT CHAIN

When a thought enters your mind as you meditate, you will be drawn to go further with it—thoughts naturally form part of an endless chain of cause and effect. If such a thought chain is triggered (see below), you don't have to follow it. You can choose to exit by bringing awareness of your breathing to the foreground, seeing the thought from the outside for exactly what it is—just a thought.

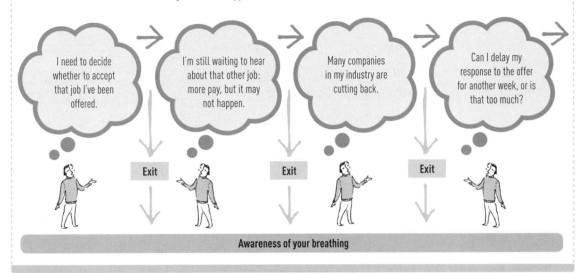

I need to decide whether to accept that job I've been offered.

I'm still waiting to hear about that other job: more pay, but it may not happen.

Many companies in my industry are cutting back.

Can I delay my response to the offer for another week, or is that too much?

Exit

Exit

Exit

Awareness of your breathing

emotions—they could relate to some deep issues in your life, interwoven with all kinds of anxieties or fears. You could think of these thought-complexes as heavier clouds that seem more reluctant to drift away. The approach you take in your meditation, though, will be the same: simply observing your thoughts without getting engaged in their story, and then gently returning your attention to your chosen focus.

> The moment you notice a thought and "wake up" is a moment of mindfulness.

MAKING AN ELEPHANT DISAPPEAR

Think of an elephant.

Now consciously try to "unthink" it away.

It's impossible, of course.

You can't make thoughts go away by engaging with them.

To make the elephant disappear, wiggle your toes and think about how that feels.

It's likely, while you're thinking about your toes, that the elephant, unhappy about being ignored, will simply slink away.

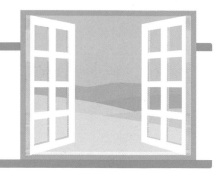

INNER WINDS
LETTING GO OF EMOTIONS

If thoughts are like clouds, emotions are like winds, pushing those clouds along on a current of feeling. In a mindfulness meditation you stand back from your emotions and feelings, while accepting them as part of your experience.

Emotions are involuntary reactions to situations. You might see your partner joking happily with someone else, and if there are already fault lines in your relationship, you might feel pangs of jealousy. Or your neighbor might start building a shed in their backyard at 7am on a Sunday, and you may feel annoyance at the banging and sawing noises. Emotions are often out of proportion to their cause: in your rational mind, you know that the jealous twinges you feel about your partner are completely groundless—there's nothing between them. And emotions persist, sometimes long after their stimulus has vanished: so you might remember your neighbor's intrusion into your Sunday morning on the following day, and feel a rising tide of anger.

Moving back to your focus
You can try to push away your emotions or to escape from them; these approaches might offer some temporary relief but are unlikely to help in the long-term. Another option is to drown out the emotions by immersing yourself in some kind of binge—drink, drugs, or food—an approach that's not only ineffective in the end but also positively harmful. All these kinds of avoidance merely create suffering, and prevent us from living fully.

ACCEPTING AN EMOTION

Instead of turning away from your emotions in avoidance, you can learn, in meditating, to gently turn toward your experience. You can bring a compassionate open attention toward the hurts you are suffering, and make wise choices in the light of your discoveries.

This involves accepting an emotion—not detaching yourself from it, but holding in awareness the feeling that it gives you. This is the opposite of punishing yourself for having the feeling: instead, with self-compassion, you open to the feeling, accepting it without wrestling with it.

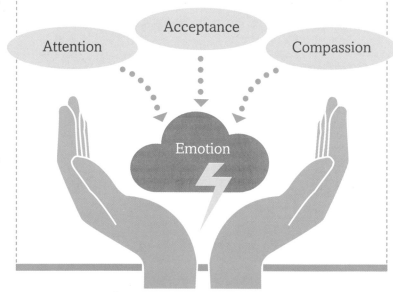

How can I be stronger than my emotions?

You can't. Open up to your emotions instead. This creates a mental space where you can witness them fully—and not be them.

EMOTIONAL RESPONSE
Nonreactive, compassionate awareness helps you deal with powerful emotions.

Avoiding, stifling, or escaping from our emotions merely creates suffering, and prevents us from living fully.

Mindfulness provides an alternative to avoidance—acceptance (see box, left). Here, you identify and acknowledge the emotion, embracing it without judgement. In a mindfulness meditation based on attending to your breathing, when emotions arise you deal with them as you deal with thoughts (see pages 100–101): you step outside them, notice them, and settle your present-moment attention once more on your chosen focus.

Learning from emotions

You can also use emotions themselves as your chosen focus in a mindfulness meditation (see pages 138–41). When you're sufficiently accepting of the emotions you experience, you can start to discern what caused them and in this way use them as a source of wisdom about yourself. These are the types of insights that contribute to deep levels of self-understanding.

HOW ARE EMOTIONS DIFFERENT FROM FEELINGS?

Imagine a zookeeper offers you a snake to handle. You have two conflicting emotions: excitement and fear. Absorbing these battling emotions, you approach the snake with caution. Your fear was an emotion; your caution is a feeling. Look at the table below to understand how emotions differ from feelings.

EMOTIONS	FEELINGS
Tell us what we like and dislike.	Tell us how to act.
Tell us to respond to life's experiences.	Tell us to respond to our emotions.
Arc immediate, instant.	Are long-term, settled.
Are intense and more fleeting.	Are low-key and more lasting.

EXAMPLES	EXAMPLES
Anxiety.	Worry.
Joy.	Happiness.
Anger.	Bitterness.
Sadness.	Depression.

WHAT'S NOT TO LIKE?
LETTING GO OF JUDGEMENT

When you're in "doing" mode, in everyday life, the mind judges things as good or bad, right or wrong, important or unimportant, urgent or nonurgent... and so on. In "being" mode, such as in a mindfulness meditation, all judgements like this are suspended.

We often find it difficult to just accept what passes through our minds. Let's look at this through a simple example. Imagine you feel resentment toward a friend who's been showered with accolades for success in some pursuit, such as art or sports. Resentment is an unpleasant emotion to have, not only in itself, but because you know it's unattractively mean-spirited. You know that the intense envy you feel is unworthy of you, and the result is that you feel bad about yourself.

Chances are that you'll recognize this destructive type of emotional pattern in your life: it's a vicious cycle of feeling bad about feeling bad. You may have experienced this too with anxiety—being anxious makes you feel that you can't cope, which leads to more anxiety. Likewise, being depressed is likely to make you feel more depressed.

Meditate and observe
In mindfulness meditation, you attend to your present-moment experience nonjudgementally. If you can do this

successfully, you'll start to dissolve the vicious and destructive cycle of self-judgement. The attitude you take if you're being mindful is acceptance—you notice and acknowledge your envy and resentment, but you don't berate yourself for feeling it.

In your meditation you've chosen to enter a zone of nonjudgement. Your role, then, is to observe with compassion, as if the person showing the resentment were a beloved friend—your troubled self, observed by your meditating self. Part of this observation is identifying how and where the experience of envy and resentment is manifesting itself. Is it purely mental or are you feeling something in your body too? Is there tension in your muscles? If so, where? Is your heart beating more quickly, or have you started to feel hot and flushed? Or are you experiencing

> The emotions I feel when meditating are powerful. I find it hard to see them in their true perspective.

> You're bigger than your emotions. They don't fill you, they travel through you.

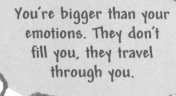

PERSPECTIVE
Remember—what you feel and what you think are not you.

the envy as a kind of reaching out in your mind for the scenario you think should be yours?

Now attend to how the emotions present themselves in your body—how your body feels. This helps you avoid getting drawn into thoughts about the emotion—don't ask why, but what. What is my present moment experience of this feeling? What is my relationship to it? Is it uncomfortable?

In meditating like this, we are being not defensive, but caring toward ourselves. How do we show that we care? Simply by attending in the present moment to our experience. We're giving ourselves the gift of our own mindful attention.

All's OK

It's easier to develop acceptance if you attend to your emotions in a spirit of amicable curiosity. If you find this helps, you can say "OK" to yourself if you want—short for "It's OK for me to feel like this." It can also be a good idea to adopt a kind of inner smile—a mental expression of relaxed warmth. In this way you replace the aversion you have to an unpleasant feeling with a more creative response that doesn't set off a chain-reaction of discomfort.

> We know our envy is unworthy of us, and that makes us feel bad about ourselves.

THE CYCLE OF JUDGEMENT

Negative emotions are part of the human psyche and they often sustain themselves in a cycle of judgement (below). Mindfully accepting emotions with a friendly curiosity dissolves the cycle of feeling bad about bad feelings.

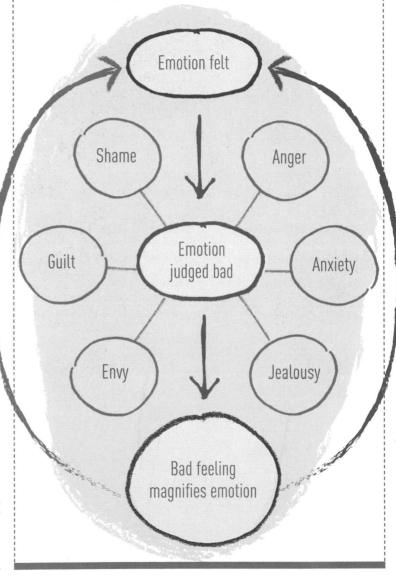

I LIVE HERE
STEP-BY-STEP BODY-AND-BREATH PRACTICE

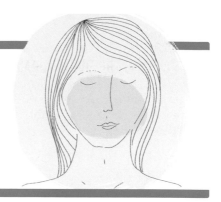

Your body offers up sensations all the time you're conscious. Usually, you ignore them—you don't register, for example, the feeling of your shirt cuff rubbing on your wrist. However, attending to such experiences grounds your mindfulness practice in the here and now and is an excellent focus for meditation.

In this simple mindfulness meditation, you will attend to body sensations in a state of relaxed and alert awareness. Sitting comfortably, in a position of relaxed stillness and stability—what some people call "sitting tall"—you'll explore your body sensations with your mind.

Ebbs and flows of sensation
The meditation described on the following pages encourages you to attend to sensations in a particular order—first one leg, then the other, for example—but there's no need to worry about following the instructions to the letter. The spirit of the exercise is what's important—that and the guidance given on what to do about mental distractions. As you gradually attend to the sensations of the body, they will form, dissolve (as you turn to the next focus) and then perhaps reform.

Many people wonder how to deal with the apparent randomness of this ebb and flow of sensation. What if one of the areas you've moved on from starts to claim your attention again? The answer is that it doesn't matter. Don't worry either if there are no sensations at all in a particular body area: willing sensations to form is not part of your purpose. Just attend to whatever you find, with complete acceptance, letting go of any wish that anything at all was otherwise.

Allow your body and its sensations to be as they are when you find them. You're like a cartographer mapping the body's terrain. Aim for complete acceptance of whatever is discovered—areas of tension, areas of numbness, aging body parts, uncooperative body parts. Let go of your wish to change anything. You're not trying to create an experience, you're registering what is actually present in the moment. This true perception of things as they are, even as a momentary experience, is deeply nourishing.

HOW DID IT FEEL?
The body is the home of your senses, and this meditation helps you map out your home territory. Once you have completed the meditation, ask yourself the following questions. Be careful not to be self-critical in your answers: the purpose of this exercise is not to test or analyze yourself but to verbalize what you were doing, which can be informative.

- When thoughts arose, were you able to meet them with curiosity and gentle awareness and let them go?

- When emotions arose, were you able to move attention to the body to notice how these emotions were experienced physically?

- Did spending some time gently focusing on your body sensations and on the movement of your breath allow these elements to be more available for your attention later in the day?

OVERCOMING THE FIVE HINDRANCES

In traditional meditation practice, the "Five Hindrances" (see below) are the major forces in the mind that impede our ability to see clearly or to concentrate fully. They are universal experiences of the adult mind. By turning a hindrance into your object of meditation, and treating it with friendly curiosity, you can prevent it from taking power over you. Follow the procedure below.

3

SLEEPINESS AND DULLNESS
Dreaminess, lack of focus, a clouded mind.

2

AVERSION
Judgement, ill-will, pushing away experiences.

4

RESTLESSNESS AND WORRY
Restless body or mind, agitation, lack of ease in your own skin.

Recognize and name the hindrance.

1

SENSUAL PLEASURE
Wanting more from the moment, being seduced by pleasurable sensory experiences.

Accept it.

5

DOUBT
Wondering, "Am I doing this right? Why am I doing this? Is anything happening?"

Bring gentle curiosity to it, considering how you feel it—in your body, in your emotions, and in your thoughts (including any actions it is urging you to perform).

CLEARING YOUR PATH
In some cases, just recognizing a hindrance is sufficient for it to fall away and free your path to clear thinking.

Observe it as a fleeting process, not something bound up with your identity.

continued ▶

BODY-AND-BREATH MEDITATION

This exercise is another cornerstone of mindfulness practice; it combines the introductory breathing meditation you have already met on pages 96–99 with a tour of physical sensations in your body.

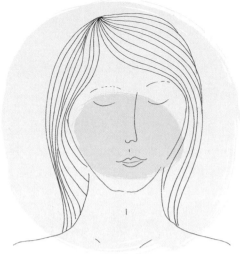

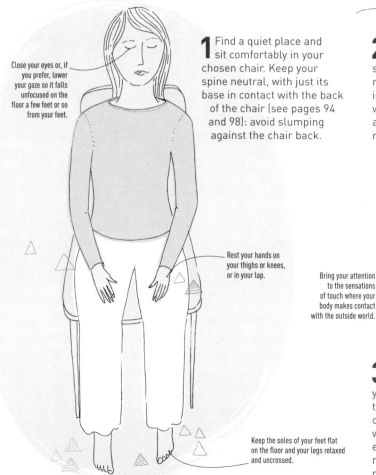

Close your eyes or, if you prefer, lower your gaze so it falls unfocused on the floor a few feet or so from your feet.

Rest your hands on your thighs or knees, or in your lap.

Keep the soles of your feet flat on the floor and your legs relaxed and uncrossed.

1 Find a quiet place and sit comfortably in your chosen chair. Keep your spine neutral, with just its base in contact with the back of the chair (see pages 94 and 98): avoid slumping against the chair back.

2 Allow your body to relax and let your mind become calm. At the same time, stay alert and aware. If you find you can't relax the first few times you try it, and this instruction is making you anxious, don't worry. Simply attend to your in-breaths and out-breaths for a minute or so, before resting your attention gently on your body.

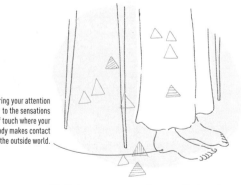

Bring your attention to the sensations of touch where your body makes contact with the outside world.

3 Bring your attention to all the places where your body is in contact with your surroundings, such as where your thighs and backs of knees touch the chair, and where your feet make contact with the floor. Spend a few seconds exploring these sensations in your mind—don't dwell too long, just make their acquaintance.

4 Now turn your attention to one foot. Start with your toes, then move to the sole of the foot, then its heel and its top. Repeat with your other foot, bringing each part briefly into awareness.

ABOUT THE PRACTICE

Benefits A core mindfulness practice, which is the next step on from the basic breath meditation. A constantly available way to connect with the present moment. It includes the breath, but extends awareness beyond that.

Frequency Do this every day for the second and third weeks of regular practice.

Duration Spend at least ten minutes on this practice, and longer if you can—15 to 20 minutes is optimum.

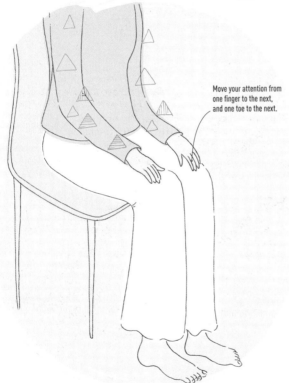

Move your attention from one finger to the next, and one toe to the next.

5 Follow the same procedure now for your legs, one after the other, and then progress from your pelvis and hips up to your shoulders, until you've explored your whole torso.

6 Now explore the sensations in your hands and arms, starting with your fingertips and working up each arm in turn to the shoulder. Then attend to the neck and the head in the same way. Spend a minute or two resting in the awareness of the whole body, just being, just breathing.

7 Attend to your breath. Focus on the sensations of each in-breath and out-breath, at your abdomen or at your nose. If you wish, put your hand on your belly to help you attend to each rise and fall. After about five minutes of mindful breathing, open your eyes and take in your surroundings again.

WHAT'S HAPPENING IN YOUR BRAIN?

THE SCIENCE OF MEDITATION

The more you meditate, the more your brain changes—for the better! Scientists are constantly adding to our knowledge of how this works. Learning about some of the important discoveries made to date can be a great motivator at this early stage in your mindfulness meditation program.

For 2,000 years people have known that meditation can deliver huge psychological benefits, but only in recent decades has modern technology been able to shed light on its likely neurological mechanisms. Researchers have used techniques that measure the frequency of electrical pulses in the brain, and those that allow areas of brain activity to be visualized, to investigate the effects of mindfulness practice. A key finding is that our brains process information less actively than usual when we meditate. In addition to these short term changes, meditation

MAPPING MEDITATION

Scientists have located several brain areas or structures associated with changes in mind-state brought about by meditative practice. This diagram shows the areas involved and describes their function.

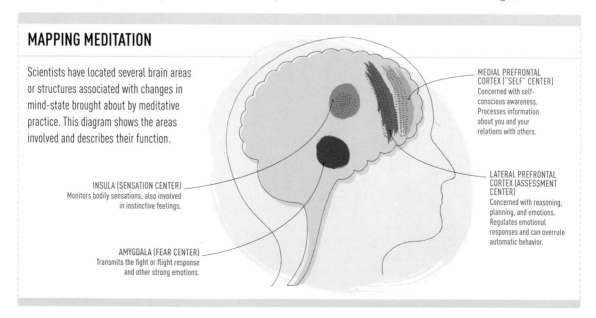

MEDIAL PREFRONTAL CORTEX ("SELF" CENTER)
Concerned with self-conscious awareness. Processes information about you and your relations with others.

LATERAL PREFRONTAL CORTEX (ASSESSMENT CENTER)
Concerned with reasoning, planning, and emotions. Regulates emotional responses and can overrule automatic behavior.

INSULA (SENSATION CENTER)
Monitors bodily sensations; also involved in instinctive feelings.

AMYGDALA (FEAR CENTER)
Transmits the fight or flight response and other strong emotions.

subtly reengineers the brain, weakening some neural connections and strengthening others, and affecting areas associated with the sense of self, empathy, and stress. Science confirms what many know to be true from direct experience of meditation—that meditators tend to take things less personally, to be less reactive to perceived threats, dangers, and discomforts, and generally to be less prone to acting on primal impulses.

These adjustments affect not only our response to sensation and emotion but also the way we see other people after meditation training—with more empathy and compassion. Some of the most important brain changes are shown in simplified form in the diagram below.

Staying power

Although these improvements are potentially long-term, that depends to some extent on the continuation of

your practice. Unless you build regular meditation into your life, the brain will probably slip back before long to its former characteristics. (This is an example of neuroplasticity—the adaptability of the brain in response to the activities it's asked to perform.) By continuing to meditate, you'll consolidate your new neural pathways—and your brain will serve you well in keeping the benefits of mindfulness at the center of your life.

THE EFFECTS OF MEDITATION

Practicing mindfulness can change the way in which our brains process fear and sensation. The brain areas and functions relate to those shown on the diagram opposite.

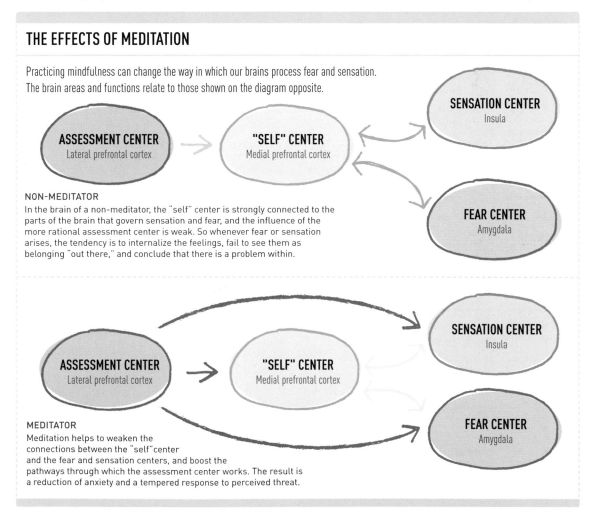

ASSESSMENT CENTER
Lateral prefrontal cortex

"SELF" CENTER
Medial prefrontal cortex

SENSATION CENTER
Insula

FEAR CENTER
Amygdala

NON-MEDITATOR
In the brain of a non-meditator, the "self" center is strongly connected to the parts of the brain that govern sensation and fear, and the influence of the more rational assessment center is weak. So whenever fear or sensation arises, the tendency is to internalize the feelings, fail to see them as belonging "out there," and conclude that there is a problem within.

ASSESSMENT CENTER
Lateral prefrontal cortex

"SELF" CENTER
Medial prefrontal cortex

SENSATION CENTER
Insula

FEAR CENTER
Amygdala

MEDITATOR
Meditation helps to weaken the connections between the "self" center and the fear and sensation centers, and boost the pathways through which the assessment center works. The result is a reduction of anxiety and a tempered response to perceived threat.

Attending mindfully and
with friendly curiosity to
sensations can help break the
cycle in which you struggle
with the reality of suffering.

HELLO LEAF, HELLO COIN
MEDITATING ON OBJECTS

Focusing mindfully on an object in a meditation is a good way to ground yourself in present experience and appreciate life's sensory richness. It complements body-and-breath practice as an occasional add-on—or just try it for a change.

There's nothing limiting or narrow-minded about choosing your own body as the focus of mindfulness meditation. The practice is self-centered only in the neutral, nonjudgemental sense of that term. Our whole lives have the self at their center, and all our thoughts and perceptions, and all the contributions we can make to our own and other people's lives, start here.

Neither is focusing on the body superficial, since our sensations are the mirror of what's going on in our lives, for good or ill. Muscular tension, for example, may have something to say about our self-esteem, or our lifestyle, or our relationships. All our body sensations are worthy of our mindful attention.

However, there's another form of mindfulness practice in which you apply nonjudgemental attention externally—to something other than your own body. This may be any object, humble or beautiful, natural or artificial. The purpose of your session is not to appreciate its objective beauty or its historical significance, but simply to attend to what you can perceive with your senses, in a spirit of neutral observation. In such meditation, you explore every aspect of an object, using all your senses in turn. If it's a fruit, you can finish your exploration by eating it—which opens up a whole new dimension of experience.

When teaching his Mindfulness-Based Stress Reduction Program, Jon Kabat-Zinn used a raisin to introduce object-based meditation to his classes. He chose this most ordinary thing, which rarely receives individual attention but is part of a large collective group, to make an important point—that meditation isn't something elevated above real life, above the detail of the world. It is a closer engagement with it.

Extended awareness

Whatever item you choose as the focus for your object-based mindfulness meditation, systematically exploring its features—its colors, shape, smell, and texture—will extend your awareness into the world outside yourself. By meditating on an object, you change your existing relationship with the world, no longer taking anything for granted. Object meditation lets you see things anew, with mindfulness.

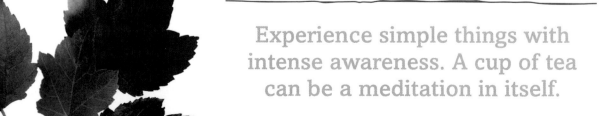

Experience simple things with intense awareness. A cup of tea can be a meditation in itself.

REALM OF THE SENSES

Meditating on a phenomenon has a long history behind it: in Eastern meditation the focus is often a candle flame. But since mindfulness is concerned with all the senses, an object you can handle and even taste offers richer possibilities. Try a simple meditation using a cherry or any other small fruit. Attend mindfully to all its sensory dimensions. You'll be surprised how much there is to explore.

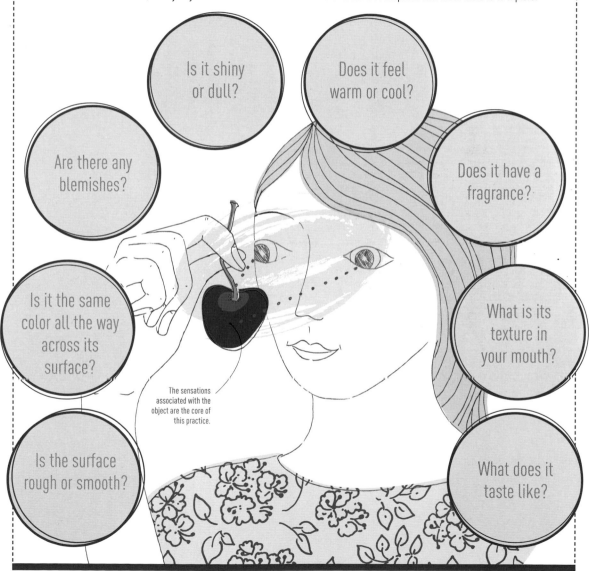

Is it shiny or dull?

Does it feel warm or cool?

Are there any blemishes?

Does it have a fragrance?

Is it the same color all the way across its surface?

What is its texture in your mouth?

The sensations associated with the object are the core of this practice.

Is the surface rough or smooth?

What does it taste like?

continued ▶

PERCEIVING A LEAF

Aesthetic appraisal is not what you are seeking in this meditation. Your purpose instead is to open your senses to an object's perceptible characteristics. However, that does not mean that relishing beauty has no part in mindfulness. On the contrary, being awakened to the world around you will make you notice beauty more keenly.

OBJECTS FOR MEDITATION

Many natural objects make a good focus for meditation. Try stones, crystals, pebbles, shells, acorns, pinecones, twigs, feathers, flowers, fruit, or vegetables.

1 Pick up a fallen leaf in your yard or local park. Hold the leaf in the palm of your hand. Notice how it feels against your skin. Perhaps there are some places where it touches you and some places where it does not?

Let the leaf lie on your hand without manipulating it: notice its weight.

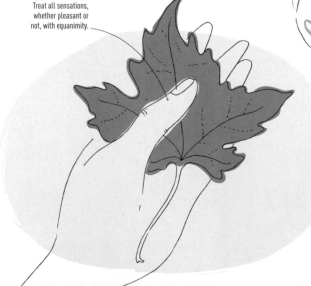

Treat all sensations, whether pleasant or not, with equanimity.

2 Now pick up the leaf between your thumb and your fingers. Attend to its temperature: does it feel noticeably warm or cool? Are there variations in temperature over its surface? Can you feel the leaf warming or cooling as you hold it?

3 Concentrate on the leaf's texture. Does it feel rough or smooth? Are there scratchy parts? How do the edges feel compared with the center? Is it hard or soft to the touch? Firm or limp? Damp or dry? How does the stalk feel?

If you are outdoors, observe how the leaf bends in the breeze.

4 Follow the contours of the leaf with your eye. Observe its shape and size. Look at the leaf from different angles as you turn it in your hand, and watch its shape change.

ABOUT THE PRACTICE

Benefits Occasional mindfulness practice. May also be used as a starter meditation. It serves as an antidote to preconceptions about everyday objects. Extends focus to the body's sensations of things.

Frequency Add this to your regular practice or use it as an occasional variation.

Duration Spend five to 15 minutes meditating on a simple object.

5 Notice the hue of the leaf's upper side. Are there any variations in color or shade? Observe the details. Are there any ridges, veins, or patterns? Is the leaf blemished? Look in this way at every part of the leaf's upper side, including the stalk. Turn the leaf over and examine the underside in the same way. Is it paler or darker underneath? What markings does it have?

6 Now hold the leaf just under your nose and see if you can detect a smell. If so, savor it without trying to put a name to it or comparing it with anything. Do different parts of the leaf smell differently?

Notice where in your nose you seem to detect the leaf's smell.

PERCEIVING A COIN

Man-made objects, such as coins, may be very old and when handling them it is tempting to speculate about their history. In a mindfulness meditation, you should put these thoughts away. Concentrate solely on the object—its colors, shapes, textures, tactile qualities, and even its smell.

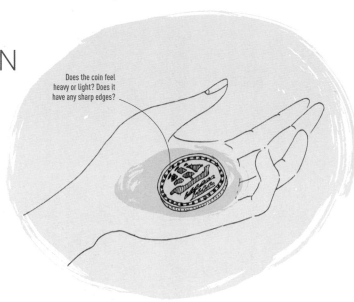

Does the coin feel heavy or light? Does it have any sharp edges?

OBJECTS FOR MEDITATION

Try this meditation with any man-made object. It should be small enough for you to view without moving, and have details big enough to see without straining your eyes—buttons, keys, stamps, and jewelry are ideal.

1 Choose a coin; it needn't be valuable or have any special associations. You can pick any coin from your pocket or purse. Hold the coin in the palm of your hand. Notice how it feels against your skin, but don't pursue thoughts about the coin. Just observe—avoid putting any labels on what you see and feel.

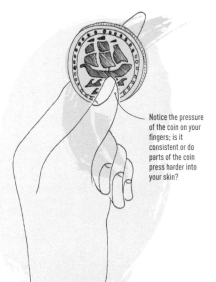

Notice the pressure of the coin on your fingers; is it consistent or do parts of the coin press harder into your skin?

ABOUT THE PRACTICE

Benefits Occasional mindfulness practice. May also be used as a starter meditation. It serves as an antidote to preconceptions about everyday objects. Extends focus to the body's sensations of things.

Frequency Add this to your regular practice or use it as an occasional variation.

Duration Spend five to 15 minutes meditating on a simple object.

2 Pick up the coin between your thumb and your fingers. Register its temperature: does it feel noticeably warm or cool? Can you feel it warming or cooling as you hold it?

3 Turn your attention to the coin's texture. Does it feel smooth or does it have a surface in deep relief? How distinct is the edge? Is there a milled pattern around the circumference? If so, does this feel fine or coarse?

4 Look closely at the coin's shape and size. Turn it in your hands, and watch its shape change as you handle it. Notice the color of the coin's metal. Is the surface shiny or dull? Are there any variations in color or shade? How worn are the surfaces and edges?

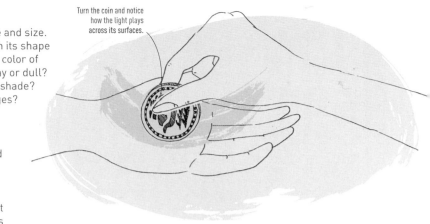

Turn the coin and notice how the light plays across its surfaces.

5 Observe the details of the head side (if there is one). Is the head young, old, or middle-aged? What items of clothing are shown? What other features? Don't attempt to identify the person shown, but don't be concerned if his or her identify is known to you: just let that thought pass away as you continue looking.

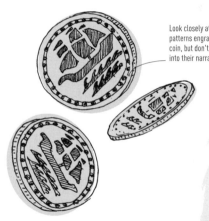

Look closely at the patterns engraved in the coin, but don't get drawn into their narrative.

6 Turn over the coin and examine the obverse side in the same way. What is depicted, and in what way? Just register what you see: ignore any symbolic associations you recognize.

7 Now lift the coin to your nostrils and see if you can detect a smell. If so, experience it without trying to put a name to it or trying to imagine what caused it.

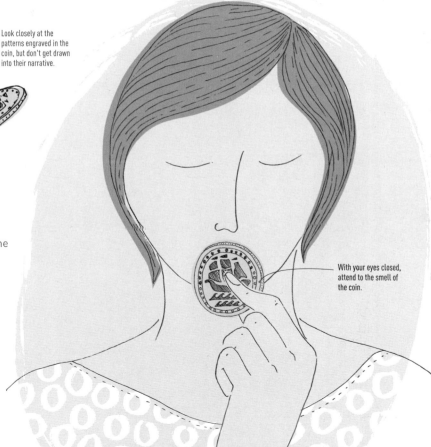

With your eyes closed, attend to the smell of the coin.

BODY SCAN BASICS
PHYSICAL SELF-AWARENESS

This wonderfully nourishing exercise is one of the mainstays of mindfulness practice. You attend to each part of your body in turn with maximum self-awareness, noticing the sensations and emotions that reside there. The result is a harmonization of body and mind into an integrated whole.

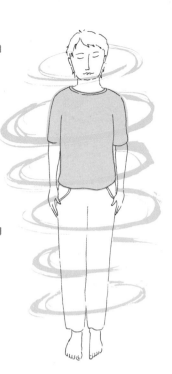

FINDING A COMFORTABLE POSITION

You can practice body scan meditation when sitting or standing, but most people prefer to lie down on a bed, mat, or a rug. Lying in one position for 30 minutes or more can be a challenge: if you feel cold, cover yourself with a light blanket; and shift your body position slowly and mindfully until you are comfortable.

STAYING ALERT

The body scan isn't a relaxation exercise. Even so, you might well fall asleep while doing it. Don't judge yourself if this happens. Propping up your head with a pillow, or keeping your eyes open, or even doing a sitting version of the practice will help you stay awake if you feel drowsy.

Try placing a pillow or a folded towel under your head to keep comfortable but alert.

Bending and lifting your knees, or resting them on a pillow, can help keep you comfortable.

When practicing body scan mindfulness meditation, you attain spacious awareness by shifting your attention slowly around your body, region by region, like training a flashlight around the walls of a cave.

You cannot hold the whole body in the mind at once, since the mind is unable to multitask: it can only work sequentially. As your focus moves from one area to the next, you will become aware of bare physical sensations, such as pulsing, tension, heaviness, burning, stiffness, and so on, and you may also recognize emotions that reside within your body. You hold these sensations without judgement or reaction; as you do so, you may find that they subside in intensity.

Continued practice helps to strengthen your capacity to pay sustained attention. At the same time, you're opening yourself up to self-compassion because the attention you direct onto the body is friendly and caring, as well as curious.

Central practice

The body scan is the core practice in many mindfulness programs (see pages 90–91) where it often follows a period of breathing and body-and-breath meditations. Try doing it twice a day for a whole week—perhaps with a rest day when you do something less disciplined, such as an object meditation. There will inevitably be times when you can't fit in a body scan because of pressing commitments or lack of energy; don't judge yourself— move on to the next day.

> The body scan is a nourishing practice; try it when you feel tired or demotivated. You'll be pleased you summoned up the will to do it.

BREATHING INTO BODY AREAS

As you turn your attention to each area of the body in turn, try imagining your breath traveling through your body to that area as you breathe in, and then leaving the area again as you breathe out. As you do this, imagine the sensations in that part of the body being gently soothed. This, of course, is not how your anatomy works, but to visualize the process in this way can help to make the body scan a more harmonized, integrated experience.

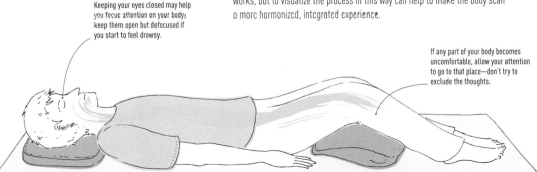

Keeping your eyes closed may help you focus attention on your body; keep them open but defocused if you start to feel drowsy.

If any part of your body becomes uncomfortable, allow your attention to go to that place—don't try to exclude the thoughts.

continued ▶

BODY SCAN MEDITATION

The body scan requires a substantial commitment of at least 30 minutes per session—ideally up to 45 minutes. As with any mindfulness practice, the idea is to be aware of your experience in the present, and without judgement.

> **MOVING ON**
>
> It's perfectly normal for you to feel no sensation from some parts of your body. If this happens, just rest your awareness in these areas briefly as the breath comes and goes, attending to the absence of sensation, before gently moving on.

1 Lie down on your back with legs slightly apart. Raise your knees if that's more comfortable. Close your eyes—but feel free to open them any time if that feels better. Feel the weight of your body on the mat or bed and notice where your body is touching the sheet or the mat.

Focus for two or three minutes on the sensations of breathing in your abdomen as it lifts and sinks in a regular rhythm.

2 When you feel ready, move your awareness to the toes of your left foot. Focus on each toe in turn. Be aware of any sensations—the touch of one toe against another, warmth or coldness, or any tingling feelings. Then turn your awareness to the other parts of the left foot—the sole, then the ball, the heel, the top and both sides of the foot, and finally the ankle.

3 Now move your attention, in turn, to your left shin, calf, knee, and thigh, scanning each area with your awareness for about half a minute, then letting go and moving to the next area. Be sure to do the calf and thighs on all sides.

4 When you feel ready, take your attention away from your left leg and on to your right leg. Focus on each toe in turn as before, and then progress to the sole, ball, heel, top and sides, and ankle. Move your attention in turn to the right calf, knee, and thigh.

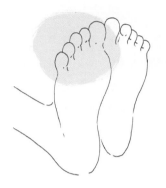

ABOUT THE PRACTICE

Benefits A core mindfulness practice and the next step from the body-and-breath meditation. It brings mind and body together as an integrated whole and is deeply nourishing when done consistently within a program of practice.

Frequency Do this twice a day for at least a week, or alternatively do one longer session per day. You can allow yourself one day off per week, perhaps doing an object meditation instead.

Duration It will take you at least 30 minutes, allowing about half a minute per body part, but ideally set aside 45 minutes.

5 Follow the same procedure now for your pelvic region—groin, genitals, buttocks, and hips, taking your time over each area. When you're ready, move to the lower torso, lower abdomen, and lower back. Be aware of your abdomen moving as you breathe.

Be mindful of any emotions that reside in the different parts of your body.

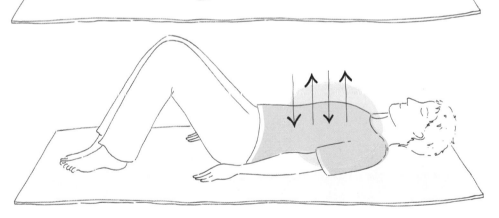

6 Focus your attention on your chest and upper back, bringing awareness to the rise and fall of your rib cage in rhythm with your breathing. Attend to your heart beating if you can feel it. Be aware of your lungs in action.

continued ▶

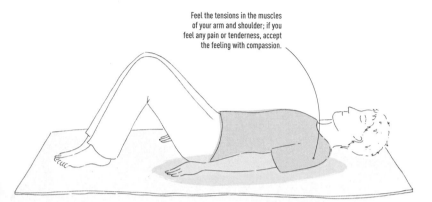

Feel the tensions in the muscles of your arm and shoulder; if you feel any pain or tenderness, accept the feeling with compassion.

9 Be aware of your eyes and eyelids—another important source of sensation. Feel your blinking, and notice any difference in sensation between one eye and the other. Attend to your nose, feeling your in-breaths and out-breaths.

7 Take your attention down your left arm, and focus on the thumb and fingers, just as you did the toes. Then do the palm, the wrist, the back, and the sides of the hand. Travel up the left arm, attending in turn to the lower arm, elbow, upper arm and shoulder. Follow the same procedure for your right thumb, fingers, hand, arm, and shoulder.

8 Next, focus your attention on your neck and throat. After half a minute or so, move to your jaw and attend to your mouth—a major source of sensation within the body. Feel your lips touching, and any adhesion there. Feel the wetness, and where its limits are. Feel your tongue against your teeth and the roof of your mouth.

Bring attention to the muscles of the jaw. Notice the warmth or coldness of your nose and ears.

DEALING WITH UNCOMFORTABLE SENSATIONS

As you move your attention through your body, you may experience some uncomfortable sensations. Try attending to them in a neutral way—curious, receptive, allowing. The process outlined here explains how mindful awareness of these sensations overturns our habit of avoiding them. Facing them, with friendly awareness in the moment, we find they aren't permanent.

We have cravings and aversions—things we deeply wish will happen and things we deeply wish won't happen.

Body scans train us in acceptance—in letting things be as they are and offering ourselves and our bodies a compassionate attention, which we can then extend to others.

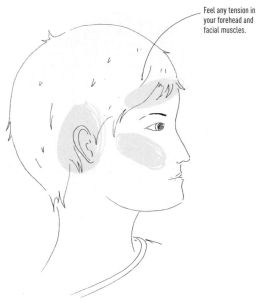

Feel any tension in
your forehead and
facial muscles.

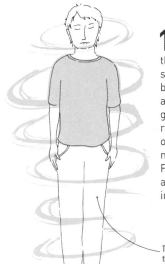

11 After scanning your body area by area in this way, conclude by spending a few minutes being aware of your body as a whole, as your breath gives it life, in its perpetual rhythm of inflow and outflow. Leave the meditation gently. Feel your completeness as a person, at peace in stillness.

Thank yourself for
the time you have
spent attending to your
own body.

10 Focus in turn on your ears, cheeks, temples, forehead, and then the back and top of your head, including your hair as it rests against the skin.

CONTINUED NONJUDGEMENT

As with all other mindfulness meditations, notice any stray thoughts or emotions that cross your mind, or any sounds you hear, and let them go, refocusing gently on bodily sensations. After you have finished your body scan, write down your experiences in your mindfulness journal.

This is our suffering—resulting from not accepting the reality of the present moment.

Many of these cravings and aversions are unconscious, and are manifested in bodily sensations.

We avoid the unpleasant sensations and gravitate toward the pleasant ones. This reinforces our cravings and aversions—our suffering.

With sustained nonjudging awareness of an uncomfortable sensation, our relationship to it changes, and this can at times lead to changes in the sensations themselves.

We become acquainted with our bodily stresses and cultivate a more accepting, intimate relationship with them, learning more about their shifting and transitory nature.

Attending mindfully, with friendly curiosity, to our bodily sensations—in a body scan—can break this cycle of struggling with the reality of suffering.

SENSATIONAL!
ENGAGING ALL THE SENSES

The senses are the interface between self and its environment, filtering everything we perceive in the world around us. Vision and hearing tend to dominate our lives. Use these prime senses to connect to the now, but give time to the other three senses too.

Purposefully perceiving our immediate surroundings through our five senses—sight, sound, touch, smell, and taste—brings us into direct and exclusive contact with the present moment. When the senses are engaged, the mind has no time for thoughts or emotions, nor for the past or the future.

Rebalancing

At this point in our mindfulness journey, after exploring physical sensations in a body scan, it's good to reacquaint ourselves with all our senses. The body scan was largely a matter of internal sensation (bypassing the five senses), with touch and taste in certain areas. Going beyond the body into your immediate surroundings takes you, potentially, on a five-dimensional sensory safari.

Do the two exercises presented here to train your senses, one by one, in present-moment awareness. Get used to opening up all your senses in everyday life. It's a good way to ground yourself when you feel yourself drifting into unproductive thoughts.

SMELL AS THE GATEWAY TO MEMORY

Our olfactory organs pass any smell we experience to a set of structures in the brain called the limbic system, which plays a key role in controlling our moods, memories, and emotions. This is why smells often evoke memories—for example, the scent of a pinewood might bring back recollections of a childhood camping trip. And learning new things in the presence of a strong scent can help you recall them when you smell the odor again. Smells also evoke emotions—this link is exploited by the perfume industry, which produces scent evocative of qualities such as desire, vitality, and tranquillity.

You can turn olfactory stimuli into a simple mindfulness meditation. If a particular smell has a powerful effect on you, open your awareness to that effect: is it a memory or an emotion unconnected with the past? Go deeper into the association, in a spirit of self-exploration.

"The more you eat, the less flavor; the less you eat, the more flavor."
Chinese proverb

THE FIVE-POINT SENSE MEDITATION

Do this ten-minute meditation—two minutes per sense—at any time, anywhere you like. You can do it standing if that's more convenient. It's good to try this in unexpected places, to trace your sensory surroundings. You may find that your experience of the world is enriched, as you discover dimensions you miss when you're focusing solely on the most obvious perceptions of sight and sound.

TOUCH

Start by attending to the touch of your clothes on your skin, then move on to your surroundings. Touch things within reach, closing your eyes once you've found a suitable object of focus.

SIGHT

Look around you. Ignore what you know about depths and distances, instead seeing your surroundings in two dimensions, not three. Attend to colors and shades, shapes, and details. Notice the divisions between things.

SMELL

Attend to distinctive aromas, if there are any. Bring suitable things, such as flowers or foods, close to your nose if not. If no smells are detectable, savor your ability to smell, while visualizing the organs of smell in your nose.

HEARING

Listen, with eyes closed, to sounds near and far. Scan the whole range of possible pitches and volumes. Listen to the sounds of your body as well as those of the external world. Note the ways in which some sounds change and fade.

TASTE

Start by tasting the inside of your own mouth. Then bite into an apple or other fruit, savoring what's distinctive about its taste. Jon Kabat-Zinn, the pioneer of modern mindfulness practice, used raisins for this taste meditation.

DESTINATION SENSE

Visit a place that offers a particularly rich landscape for one or more of the senses—for example, a busy café is full of sounds, while a spring garden offers up a multitude of scents. Find somewhere to sit and mindfully take in the superabundance of sensation.

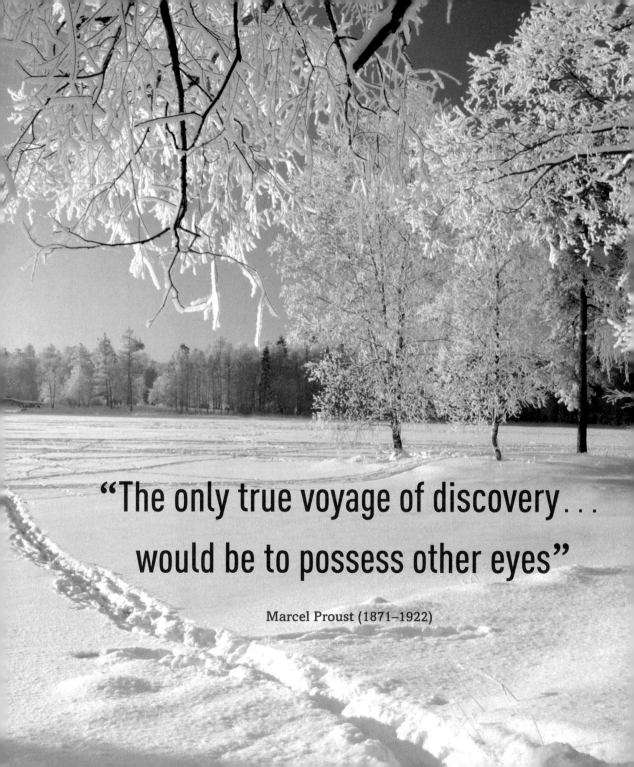

"The only true voyage of discovery...
would be to possess other eyes"

Marcel Proust (1871–1922)

YOUR INNER ROLLERCOASTER
WHEN EMOTIONS SURFACE

Emotions often gallop into your mind during mindfulness practice, like wild horses across a prairie. Attending to their flavor, without getting drawn into their stories, can be an instructive part of inhabiting the present moment.

Certain body sensations, such as a sense of heaviness or fatigue, tension in the muscles, or a round-shouldered posture, can speak volumes about our state of mind. If we feel ourselves to be lacking in vitality, self-esteem, and optimism, these physical symptoms have the effect of reinforcing our negative self-image. In other words, we get stuck in a cycle—an unhappy feedback loop. Noticing these sensations can be a way of recruiting the body as an ally in our effort to escape the negative cycle and start to move toward contentment.

Emotions observed
We may also, in the course of a mindfulness meditation, find that emotions arise quite directly—as raw feeling rather than via physical sensation. This is most likely to occur when we practice the body scan (see pages 120–25)—a long meditation in which we are likeliest to encounter the deepest experiences of the self.

Many who do the body scan meditation find themselves confronting emotions that have previously been hidden from the conscious mind, but which may have had a marked effect on their attitudes and behavior. Mindfulness provides us with a means to look at these emotions with self-compassionate acceptance. We can look at these visitations directly in the eye—not with hostility but with curiosity. Once we have acclimatized ourselves to this approach, we can go much further by rolling out the red carpet for our emotions, welcoming them into the field of our observation, and seeing how they comport themselves. This can be the beginning of a journey of self-discovery.

Dissolving negative patterns
Breaking free of established patterns of thought or behavior that are based on ingrained emotional responses is no easy feat. Taking determined action to fight these emotions is not the best way to overcome them—indeed the effect might be, paradoxically, to strengthen

MINDFUL FOCUS ON AN EMOTION

Try contemplating an emotional experience in the same way you'd contemplate a flower. Attend to it with your full awareness, taking in all its characteristics.

Imagine the emotion wants you to see it as it is. Move in as close as feels comfortable. Don't be alarmed if the emotion becomes more intense as you approach it—that's normal. Try again another time if you find the encounter overwhelming. Write down your experiences in your journal.

> ## As your mindfulness practice progresses, you'll be able to face difficult emotions more calmly and with greater acceptance.

them, because to do this, we have to confront the emotions directly in our conscious minds. What's needed is a new, more mindful way of thinking. By training ourselves to live in the present moment, and relating to our experience with acceptance rather than judgement, we become more grounded and more nimble in our responses. Autopilot dissolves when mindfulness takes over the wheel.

The flavor of acceptance

Treating your emotional difficulties with acceptance, in the present moment, does not mean resigning yourself to the negative messages they carry. Instead, it means opening up to the emotions. From a mindful perspective, these emotions don't carry banners bearing negative propaganda about you, just as positive emotions don't shout hurrahs in your favor. In a mindfulness meditation you accept positive and negative emotions with an even-handed openness.

Setting your own pace

None of this means that the body scan is a place where you have to face your demons, however unprepared you are. If you find it hard to face an emotion that arises, that difficulty becomes part of what you observe in yourself. Simply accept your own reluctance with compassion—and return to your point of focus. In your encounters with your own distress, you can choose the pace of acquaintance that seems right to you. You're in no hurry. Your main priority is to experience being in the present moment and you can gather into that experience as much recognition of your emotional state as you intuitively feel is right for you at this time.

STEPPING OFF THE ROLLERCOASTER
The experience of being on a rollercoaster is very different to one of observing a rollercoaster from a distance. Mindfulness can give you that distance.

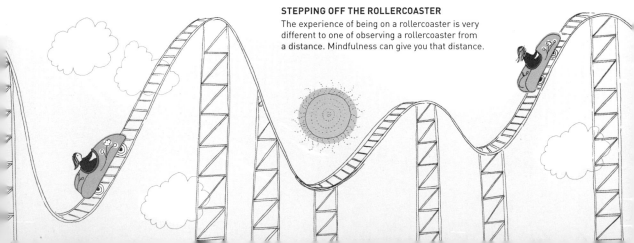

TAKE IT IN YOUR STRIDE
A STEP-BY-STEP WALKING MEDITATION

Noticing how your body feels in motion is a further application of mindfulness to pure sensation. The walking meditation is a time-honored formal practice, with Zen echoes, but you can also build it less formally into your everyday life. After all, walking—even on busy city streets—is something that many of us do already.

AWARENESS TO GO

There's no particular technique to mindful walking. Don't rush—just adopt a comfortable, regular pace. If your mind strays, attend to the feel of your feet on the ground to return to the desired state. To introduce some variety into your practice, try some of the simple projects shown here. Think of them as excursions that can enhance your walking meditation, help connect you more vitally with your surroundings, and allow you to nurture your appreciation of your self and of your environment.

SWITCH YOUR ATTENTION
Alternate between focusing on your bodily sensations and what you perceive around you—perhaps progressing from sight to hearing, then touching anything suitable you see, then attending to any smells.

WEATHER WALK
Dress appropriately for a walk in interesting weather and experience it through all your senses. Savor such pleasures as the crunch and resistance of snow, the look of sunbeams penetrating dark clouds, the color gradations in a rainbow, or the feel of rain on your face.

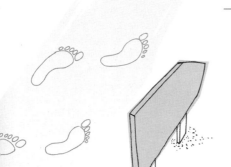

> ## "The mind can go in a thousand directions, but on this beautiful path, I walk in peace. With each step, the wind blows."
> Thich Nhat Hanh

Walking, unlike breathing, is learned—but we learned to walk so long ago that it doesn't feel like a skill at all; more like an inbuilt reflex. When we walk, we're mostly in automatic pilot mode—and given that we're navigating too, the metaphor has particular relevance. While walking we can talk or, if alone, think and reflect on our problems and anxieties. In fact, many of us go on a walk specifically to sort out some difficulty, turning it around in our minds, trying to find resolution.

A very different approach to walking is to do so mindfully. You don't set out to ruminate on issues, and if they do arise in your mind, you let them go. You walk in the present moment, attending to your bodily sensations. You can carry out this meditation informally on the go, wherever you walk—on the way to the store, or to a meeting, for example. Alternatively, you can set aside time for mindful walks, building them into your formal program of body and breath meditations. You can also use informal walking meditations to add variety to your practice—take a look at the suggestions below.

SONGLINES
Go for a walk in spring, when birds are singing. Pinpoint individual birds purely from their song, aware of the sound-source shifting in relation to you as you walk. Filter overlapping sounds in your mind.

STOREWALKER
Visit a department store and take the escalators to the top floor, observing the abundance and variety of merchandise of all kinds from a changing angle. Watch and listen to people as well, and hear the sounds of shopping.

FROM ALL SIDES
Visit a building that stands self-contained in its grounds—perhaps a museum or church in a public park. Walk around the building paying close attention, in the moment, to all its features and characteristics, and the way your view changes.

continued ▶

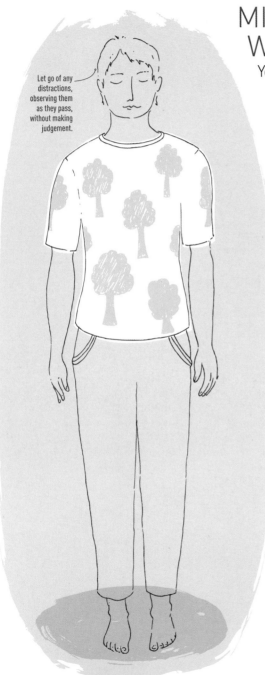

Let go of any distractions, observing them as they pass, without making judgement.

MINDFULNESS WALKING MEDITATION

You can do this meditation indoors or out. Indoors, you don't need a large room, as you can walk in circles, or back and forth, within a small one—though it might help to clear some furniture out of the way. Walking barefoot is good for increased sensitivity, if you're walking on a carpet or other comfortable surface.

1 Stand upright in a stable position, arms hanging by your sides. Be aware of your feet in contact with the ground; you might like to visualize yourself as a tree—grounded, majestic, tall. Move your body around a little until you find the sweet spot of perfect balance.

2 Focus on your breathing for a minute or two. Then, when you're ready, shift your attention to your feet.

ABOUT THE PRACTICE

Benefits Extends body and breath mindfulness to a new dimension—movement.

Frequency Entirely optional. If you find the practice rewarding you could do it daily. Or you might prefer to use it as an occasional variation within a routine of body-and-breath meditations or full body scans.

Duration Ten minutes or so is recommended, but do it for longer if you wish.

3 Move your weight over onto one foot, so there's hardly any weight on the other. Then press down on the weight-bearing foot, relax the other knee, move that leg forward, sway your body as necessary to keep your balance, and feel the heel and ball of the other foot rolling on the floor.

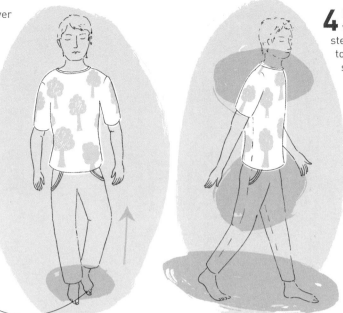

Move slowly and purposefully with full awareness of all the sensations involved.

4 Do the complementary version of this first step, with alternate feet, to perform the second step, in a forward motion. Attend to all the sensations of movement in your legs, feet, and upper body, and to the pressure on the foot and its contact with the floor.

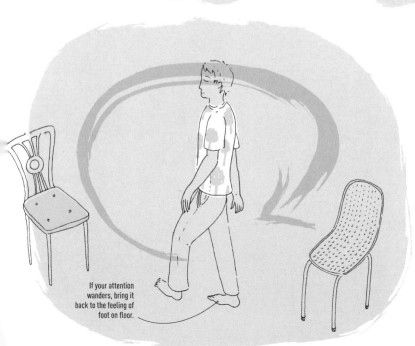

If your attention wanders, bring it back to the feeling of foot on floor.

5 Repeat the rhythm of slow, deliberate walking, all the time attending to the sensations as they unfold, and noticing the repeated sensations, as well as any changes. Walk forward or turn as necessary, within the confines of your space.

VARIATIONS

Try walking to your breaths. Breathe out as you take one foot forward; breathe in while moving the other foot. Use the rhythm of your breathing to regulate your steps.
Try a walking body scan. Shift your awareness as you walk, starting with your feet and moving up to the top of your head (see the body scan, pages 120–25).

"People usually consider walking on water or in thin air a miracle. But I think the real miracle is... to walk on earth."

Thich Nhat Hanh (1926–)

WAVES OF COMPASSION
A LOVING KINDNESS MEDITATION

This meditation, based on Buddhist practice, starts with *self*-compassion—the acceptance of yourself with all your quirks and flaws—and then moves on, in widening circles, to embrace others in a wave of positive energy. By generating warmth, we add to the sum of happiness—including our own.

When we start noticing that our attitudes toward other people have turned negative, and we're holding back warm feelings toward them, or even feeling a background buzz of resentment or negativity, it's time to do something about it. It might just be a few individuals we feel coldly toward; it could be specific groups, such as our bosses, or men in general; or it could be humanity as a whole.

When our minds turn sour in this way, it's certainly within our capacity to sweeten them, by stimulating empathy toward others. This is the job of the loving kindness meditation, a practice traditionally used by Buddhists to cultivate the mental habit of selfless or altruistic love. Doing this meditation, weekly, or whenever we feel our empathy needs a top-up, we train ourselves to be more patient, tolerant, generous, forgiving, and kind.

A heart meditation

In a loving kindness meditation you work on bringing yourself around from negative habits of thought to a more positive view of life that fills your whole being—and in the process you experience a kind of inner healing. You habituate yourself to empathy—a shared understanding of what others are experiencing. Empathy is what distinguishes compassion from pity. Whereas pity merely adopts and expresses an *attitude* of concern, compassion goes deeper, engaging with people's predicaments in a spirit of profound understanding and forgiving their errors and imperfections.

There's more to loving kindness, however, than identifying with people's problems; it also means reaching out to embrace their joys, achievements, good qualities, and good fortune.

Loving kindness is a "heart" meditation that offers an invaluable counterbalance to mind-orientated "insight" meditations. Look upon it not as a formal exercise, but as a way of generating friendly feelings, which you will then indiscriminately bring into all your interactions with others—in your home, your community, your workplace, and beyond.

Much of our unhappiness stems from our wish to be happy at the expense of others—not knowing that in the end that makes us feel pain.

WIDENING CIRCLES

When you carry out the loving kindness meditation you first bring the focus of attention to yourself, and then move outward, focusing on groups of people progressively further from your goodwill, as shown below. Obviously, we all compose our groups differently—the example below is just one permutation. If you have difficulty directing loving feelings toward yourself (because you are self-critical), begin the meditation by focusing on a beloved partner or friend, then attend to yourself.

Your partner   **YOURSELF**   Your best friend

Your children   Your grandparents

Your parents   Your grandchildren

CHERISHED AND BELOVED

Your teacher   Your boss

Your colleague   Your mentor

Your neighbor   **RESPECTED AND BELOVED**   Your cleaner

Your boss   Your acquaintance   Your doctor   Your neighbor

ACQUAINTED—FEELINGS NEUTRAL

Your ex-partner   Your colleague

ACQUAINTED—FEELINGS HOSTILE

continued ▶

THE LOVING KINDNESS MEDITATION

Loving kindness can be practiced in any posture, so choose a position that has worked well for your other mindfulness meditations. It's difficult to do the practice when you're tired, as it requires considerable reserves of mental energy.

1 Sit comfortably with your back upright. Keep your feet flat on the floor and your legs uncrossed. Close your eyes and allow yourself to relax. Let go of any distractions.

Your spine should be in a "neutral" self-supporting position.

ABOUT THE PRACTICE

Benefits Encourages openness and empathy and helps to strengthen your sense of connection with others.

Frequency Do at least once a week and whenever you feel negative about someone, or self-preoccupied.

Duration 30 minutes recommended.

2 Make a wish of loving kindness for yourself by silently expressing the following words: "May I experience loving kindness for myself. May I enjoy happiness, health, and peace." Feel the sincere intention of the words as you say them. Repeat them or elaborate them (adding more wishes in the same spirit) until you feel warm feelings toward yourself arising.

3 Make a wish of loving kindness to someone dearly beloved, this time silently addressing them in person—for example, "Dearest daughter, may you experience loving kindness. May you enjoy happiness, health, and peace." Again, feel the warm sincerity of the words as you say them. If you wish, include more than one person at this stage, or elaborate on specific wishes if you prefer.

4 Make a wish of loving kindness to someone beloved and respected, such as a person who has taught you something important in your life, or helped you at times of crisis. Again, choose your own form of words for this, but ideally echoing the words you used at step 3.

5 Send loving kindness to an acquaintance you have neutral feelings about. By all means address them by their name if you know it, but don't worry whether you should use their first name or their surname: what you call them is unimportant.

6 Send loving kindness to someone you dislike or who has made you angry. You will probably feel negative feelings initially, but these should fade as you continue your meditation.

COMPASS POINTS

You can extend the loving kindness meditation by sending warm feelings to humanity in general. Divide people into four groups according to their direction from you: north, south, east, and west. If you wish, turn to face these directions when you meditate. Alternatively, try focusing on the people in your city or country.

Listen, or your tongue
will keep you deaf.

Native American proverb

MINDFUL IMAGINATION
HOW TO BECOME A MOUNTAIN

This meditation brings the imagination into play—not with random thoughts, like those of a daydream, but focused purposefully in the present moment. Stretching the imagination like this helps us develop our sensitivity.

Our imagination is our ability to create a mental image of something that isn't perceived through the five senses. This image may be of some future event we fear—in which case we're using our imagination to amplify our own anxiety. Or it might be something we'd dearly love to happen—in which case we might be nurturing a delusion (if it never does happen), or at least a preconception. However, it's also possible to use the imagination mindfully, just as we can use our senses mindfully.

Daydreaming is not usually mindful, since it involves losing touch with present, purposeful awareness, and drifting off into a mental limbo. But instead of letting your imagination wander, you can, if you choose, focus it in the present moment, as you did previously with the loving kindness meditation (see pages 138–41). On the following pages is a meditation designed to make you feel grounded in the moment by inhabiting not a sensory experience but a specifically chosen imaginary experience—that of becoming a mountain.

Stable and grounded

A mountain is stable, majestic, and immune to the vagaries of weather, and this meditation helps you to find a parallel strength and stability within yourself. It reminds you that any inner storms you face—the equivalent of mountain weather—have no true bearing on the essence of your being. One of the reasons it has become so popular in mindfulness practice is that it relates directly to a seated person, in terms of pose (being still with a lowered center of gravity) and shape (it's easy to imagine your head as the peak and your arms and thighs as slopes).

It's important to develop your imagination, since it's the basis of empathy—that is, imagining how you'd feel in someone else's place. An empathic thought, like the mountain meditation, is an example of imaginary powers being focused with specific purpose.

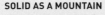

SOLID AS A MOUNTAIN
Just as a mountain is impassive to extremes of weather, we can learn to regard good and bad thoughts and feelings with equanimity.

THE POWER OF THE IMAGE

To understand the power of mental imagery, we need only think of memory: by visualizing a fact in some way, we're more likely to recall it when we need to. Focusing on an imaginary object is a common procedure in meditation.

TYPES OF VISUALIZATION

The main types of visualization used in meditation are:

- Focusing on an imagined object, such as a star or sunset.

- Focusing on an imagined scene—a tranquil lake, for example. This helps to calm the mind and ease anxiety.

- Imagining that you are something else, like a mountain or a bird. This can help you find inner qualities through the power of metaphor.

- Imagining a desirable future event. Many use this method of creative visualization, to motivate themselves.

> "Imagination is more important than knowledge. Knowledge is limited. Imagination encircles the world."
> Albert Einstein (1879–1955)

continued ▶

MINDFUL MOUNTAIN MEDITATION

Imagine the mountain in as much detail as you wish. But bear in mind that the scene-setting is less important than the power of taking the mountain into yourself. Once you've become the mountain in your imagination, visualize, less precisely, the view you'd have of neighboring mountains in the range stretching in front of you.

1 Sit comfortably on a chair, with your back upright and your spine self-supporting. Rest your hands on your thighs or in your lap. Keep your feet flat on the floor. Close your eyes.

Find a stable seated position, and notice the pressure of the chair on your body.

2 Take mindful breaths for a minute or two. You might like to imagine that your mind is full of sky—the world your mountain will inhabit.

3 Picture a mountain in front of your eyes. Imagine it in as much detail as you can. Picture the green lower slopes, with belts of conifers; above them are the rocky crags and crevices, followed by snow and ice toward the summit.

Let the mountain come into ever-sharper focus; take in both its form and its details.

BECOMING THE LANDSCAPE

Your imagination allows you to become whatever you wish; try these experiences as an alternative to the mountain.
Lake meditation The self becomes a body of water. Emotional weather troubles only the surface; the depths remain unstirred.
Tree meditation The leaves rustle in the wind but the trunk and branches never bend. You can imagine your issues as leaves falling harmlessly to the ground.

ABOUT THE PRACTICE

Benefits Like the loving kindness practice (see pages 138–41), this meditation develops your imaginative powers—important in relationships and in creativity. It encourages mental and emotional stability and helps you access your inner strength. It can help beginners who find it difficult initially to sit still.

Frequency Do this occasionally to introduce variety into your mindfulness routine, or whenever you feel stress or face a difficult challenge.

Duration 20 minutes or so is ideal, but you can extend the practice.

4 Conjure up in your mind the solid presence of the majestic mountain, grounded in the earth. Hold this image in your mind for a few minutes. Now imagine bringing the mountain inside yourself and becoming it, in a fusion of self and mountain.

Notice the weather swirling around you as you become the mountain.

5 Picture yourself being the mountain—still and tranquil as changing weather, including storms, passes across you. Observe this weather from your impregnable stronghold of rock, ice, and snow.

6 See all your internal issues, and the emotions associated with them, as part of the mountain's weather patterns. Observe the turbulence without involvement and without judgement, secure in yourself. When you're ready, picture yourself transforming back into your everyday self, taking the power of the mountain with you, as part of your inner toolkit to engage with the world.

THE HABIT OF NOW
DEVELOPING AUTO-MINDFULNESS

Everything you do in life you can do mindfully. Alongside doing meditations, it's invaluable to explore the possibilities for living more in the moment—from waking to bedtime—and weaving mindfulness into the warp and weft of your life.

When the word "practice" appears in connection with mindfulness, it is often used to refer to meditation. But the principle of awareness in the present moment that is cultivated through mindfulness can—and should—be practiced in other areas of life. Alongside your formal meditation practice you can try applying purposeful awareness to specific periods of activity—for example,

raking leaves, walking to the bus stop, or even running marathons. You may consciously apply mindful attention to your conversations with your partner or children; or you may develop an interest in a subject that calls for attention in the moment—for many, pastimes such as music (listening or playing), birdwatching, art, or photography provide a focus for mindfulness practice.

Mindfulness is capable of transforming apparently mundane experiences into meaningful ones. The question arises, to what extent is it realistic to apply mindfulness to all your activities? Would a life lived with conscious purposeful awareness of every moment of real-time experience be realistic or desirable?

Reality check

The short answer is, arguably not, and that answer is in part a response to the word "purposeful." You'll be pursuing many purposes in life, and thinking about those purposes—and attending to your own experiences is only one of them. There are plenty of times when you wish to inhabit the past

AUTO-MINDFULNESS

Turn autopilot on its head, and make mindfulness your default setting. You will become more attentive, more observant, and more fully awake. Such a mindful attitude will come to you gradually, with the help of formal and informal practice, but the following "seeds" of mindfulness are also worth planting in your life.

Breathe mindfully at frequent intervals all through the day—use this as your rest mode (for example, when you're waiting in a line, or waiting for an appointment), and just before doing something different (for example, before a meeting).

Resolve to be mindful at least once, for a minute or two, in every hour. When watching TV, be mindful between programs or during the commercial breaks.

PARALLEL PATHWAYS

The three strands of mindfulness shown here all help you to evolve a mindful disposition.

2
INFORMAL PRACTICE
Mindfulness sessions interwoven with daily life.

3
FREQUENT SELF-CUES
Entering mindfulness in the course of daily life.

1
FORMAL PRACTICE
Planned mindfulness meditations.

ALL-EMBRACING ATTITUDE
Auto-mindfulness.

or the future, rather than the present. You may wish, for example, to conjure up memories of an absent friend whose company you miss, or reconstruct in your mind a conversation with a work colleague to help you decide what attitude to take in future dealings with that person. Mindfulness would not want to discourage you from saying,

"I was thinking about you today." Nor would it wish to ban the phrase "on reflection" from the language.

A question of attitude
If you follow a mindfulness program, it's likely that regular meditation practice will come to feel increasingly "natural" and you'll

probably wish to build such formal meditations into the regular pattern of your life. Alongside this practice, you may also choose to be mindful—albeit less formally—at certain times of your own choosing, while listening to music, cooking, or doing jobs in the garden, for example.

Beyond that, your meditations will have opened up your awareness, and it's likely that you'll be focusing more than you used to on whatever activity you're engaged in. Moreover, your periods of doing will be interspersed more and more with periods of being. This is mindfulness as an attitude.

Bring awareness to aches and pains, or other body discomforts, and to your emotions whenever they surface, as well as any negative thoughts you have about yourself.

Track your journey to mindfulness in your mindfulness journal. Write about any experiences arising from your meditations, as well as from sessions of informal mindfulness.

Meditation is just the beginning of mindfulness practice. You can bring it into any aspect of your life.

SUDDENLY YOU'RE DOING YOGA!

BEYOND THE BODY SCAN

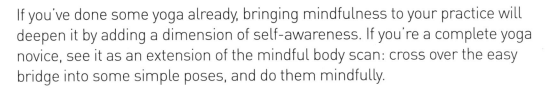

If you've done some yoga already, bringing mindfulness to your practice will deepen it by adding a dimension of self-awareness. If you're a complete yoga novice, see it as an extension of the mindful body scan: cross over the easy bridge into some simple poses, and do them mindfully.

Many people who do mindfulness practice experience it as a return to the wholeness and self-awareness that already lies deep inside themselves, awaiting rediscovery. Tuning into the body's sensations is a reconnection, not a new connection. In the body scan (see pages 120–25) each part of our body receives our compassionate attention. It isn't that the body is a temple: it's our home.

The body scan, as we've seen, applies mind to body in a way that starts to unify those two dimensions of ourselves. The idea of union also lies behind yoga, which literally means "yoking together"—a reference to the yoking of horses or oxen, which is a metaphor for mind–body harmony.

Sun and moon yoga

Yoga is an ancient practice that originated in India more than 5,000 years ago. Traditionally, it has been seen as a diving board for purification, tuning the body to receive the higher forms of meditation. Less esoterically, it's seen in its modern, Westernized variations as a way of teaching someone how to relax and release tension, strengthen weak muscles and stretch tight ones, and balance and integrate mind and body. Hatha yoga, the most common type practiced in the West today, derives its name from *ha* meaning "sun" and *tha* meaning "moon." Unifying the power of both heavenly bodies, hatha yoga releases the male and female energies within all of us. It uses traditional asanas (poses) to work on all the body's systems, offering strength and flexibility, as well as promoting healthy digestion, balancing the hormones, and calming the nerves.

Focused awareness in yoga practice allows us to perceive deep patterns of emotion and thought. From this self-understanding comes profound transformation—a fully awakened personal wholeness and wisdom. There's an obvious affinity between this process and the mechanisms of mindfulness meditations.

Mindful fusion

Whereas the yogic path, with roots in Hinduism, emphasizes concentration on the breath to take you into deep states

> Mindfulness is a way to open more deeply to your yoga practice and extend that feeling into your life as a whole.

MINDFULNESS YOGA

In recent years a number of yoga teachers, such as Frank Jude Boccio and Cyndi Lee, have been promoting the benefits of applying mindfulness to the practice of asanas (poses) in hatha yoga. Mindfulness yoga takes its mindful insights beyond the yoga mat, into the realm of everyday living—by exactly the kind of extension that we've followed in this book in moving from formal to whole-life mindfulness.

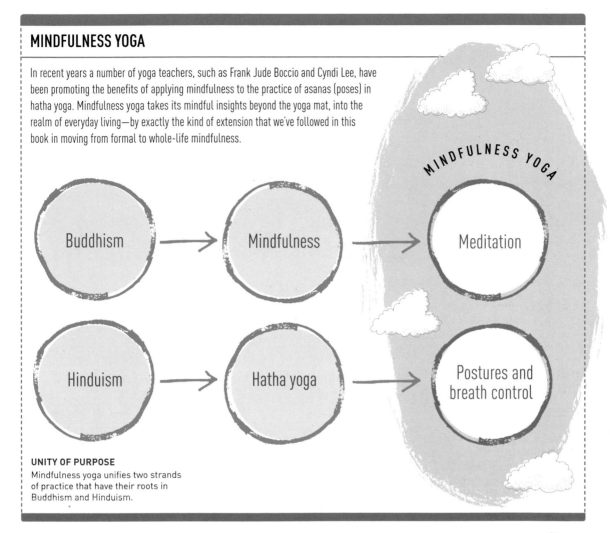

MINDFULNESS YOGA

Buddhism → Mindfulness → Meditation

Hinduism → Hatha yoga → Postures and breath control

UNITY OF PURPOSE
Mindfulness yoga unifies two strands of practice that have their roots in Buddhism and Hinduism.

of absorption, the Buddhist path focuses on mindfulness of all the experiences unfolding in your consciousness, so you can be present with whatever happens without either clinging to it or pushing it away. The two paths join at the bridge of mindful bodywork. By applying mindfulness to simple yoga poses, what you're doing is extending your body scan (see pages 120–25) into new areas of sensation.

One criticism leveled at some yoga practice has been an exaggerated emphasis on physical performance. Being able to twist the body into the more difficult positions has, for some, become a point of pride. The fusion of mindfulness with simple asanas returns yoga to its true emphasis on the whole person: the harmonization of mind and body. And to reach that point

from the body scan is just a short step forward—the first of many, hopefully, as you launch yourself on a new mindful yoga journey.

continued ▶

FOUR EASY YOGA POSES

Try each of these basic yoga poses two or three times, bringing mindful awareness to your bodily sensations. Don't do these poses if you have any issues with your lower back or neck, have arthritis, or are pregnant. Consult a yoga teacher for guidance.

MOUNTAIN POSE

In this position you stand tall and firm, like a mountain, to promote mental and physical well-being.

1 Stand tall with your arms hanging by your sides and your gaze forward. Keep your shoulders relaxed.

2 With your knees over your ankles, extend your spine and neck. Take a deep breath and raise your arms, keeping them straight.

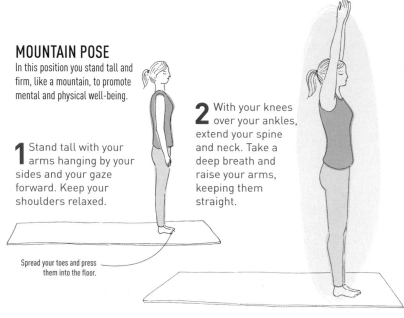

Spread your toes and press them into the floor.

MINDFUL MOVEMENTS

Any stretch or movement—even reaching up to the top shelf in a food store for a box of cereal becomes yoga when done mindfully, because you are yoking movement with awareness. Try carrying out some basic leg lifts, leg stretches, raising and dropping arms, holding your arms above your head, or any other simple movements and transforming them into a moving body scan.

CHAIR POSE

This position helps to strengthen your lower body and stretches the back.

Pull your shoulder blades firm against your back.

1 Stand with your feet hip-width apart, pointing forward. Take a deep in-breath and lift your arms straight up above your head, keeping them parallel, palms facing inward or touching.

2 Breathe out and bend at the hips, lowering yourself, as if sitting in a chair. Go down as low as you feel comfortable. Lengthen through your spine. Breathing deeply, hold this pose for six to eight breaths. Return to your standing position. Then repeat the posture.

Keep your knees pointing forward rather than to the sides.

CHILD POSE

This pose gently stretches your thighs and hips and many find its fetal position calming.

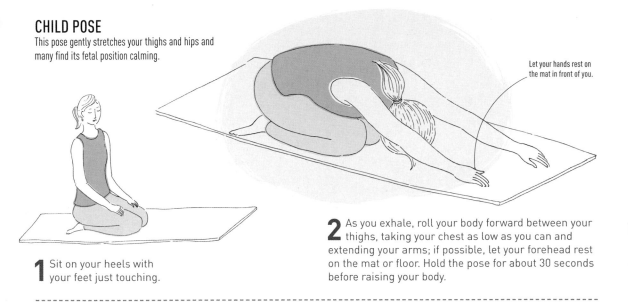

Let your hands rest on the mat in front of you.

1 Sit on your heels with your feet just touching.

2 As you exhale, roll your body forward between your thighs, taking your chest as low as you can and extending your arms; if possible, let your forehead rest on the mat or floor. Hold the pose for about 30 seconds before raising your body.

COBRA

This position stretches your upper body and back and helps to strengthen your arms and shoulders.

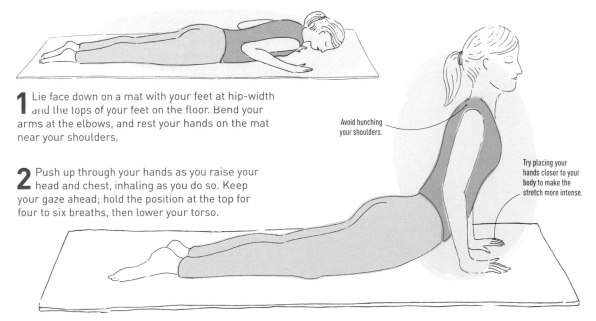

1 Lie face down on a mat with your feet at hip-width and the tops of your feet on the floor. Bend your arms at the elbows, and rest your hands on the mat near your shoulders.

2 Push up through your hands as you raise your head and chest, inhaling as you do so. Keep your gaze ahead; hold the position at the top for four to six breaths, then lower your torso.

Avoid hunching your shoulders.

Try placing your hands closer to your body to make the stretch more intense.

MINDFULNESS LIFE SKILLS

BUILDING MINDFULNESS INTO YOUR LIFE ENABLES YOU TO BECOME A MORE GROUNDED, MORE CONFIDENT, AND HAPPIER PERSON, WITH MORE FULFILLING RELATIONSHIPS.

TANGLED TALES
HOW TO PUT STRESS IN PERSPECTIVE

Stress can permeate all aspects of our lives, with its potent mix of bodily symptoms and anxious thinking. Mindfulness helps you disentangle stress-inducing thoughts and see them in a truer perspective that weakens their hold.

It can poison our happiness, blow up our bridges, block our escape routes: stress is the saboteur of modern life. It causes physiological symptoms, such as heart problems, digestive complaints, and depression that can threaten our health in the long term. It strikes when we're at our lowest—when we have financial problems or when we're seriously ill—and it thrives when we're in conflict with people, when we're going through a major life change, such as job loss or divorce, or feel trapped in a situation we can't alter. It latches on to any doubts we might have about our performance in a role—whether employee, boss, husband, wife, or carer.

Diagnosis
Stress is a self-protective mechanism that evolved to help us deal with a perceived threat, either by engaging with it or by fleeing from it—the so-called "fight or flight" response. A stress cue triggers the release of hormones, including adrenaline and cortisol, which cause physical changes, such as a raised heartbeat, which takes more blood to the muscles, priming us for action.

Similarly, "churning" of the stomach, results from blood being rerouted where it is needed.

False and true triggers
The stress response evolved far back in evolutionary history. It remains in today's developed societies, even though we rarely face life-threatening dangers. Our stress can be triggered by setbacks in our relationships or careers; it can come from our inner thoughts (see box, below); and sometimes the fight or flight response is activated when nothing serious is at stake but our ego is threatened—for example, when someone is rude or dismissive.

Mindfulness helps with the accurate appraisal of such situations and can tell us if the stressor is real. We may find, for example, that we become angry at a coworker, and that anger causes us stress. If we've taken mindfulness into our life, we'll be able to recognize that

---

KNOTWORK

Inner stress can often seem to be a huge tangled knot. Entering the moment, in a spirit of self-examination, we are able to unravel the knot and see its individual strands for what they are. Seeing the causes of inner stress with detachment, we can apply a mindful response to each strand of the knot.

INNER STRESS	MINDFUL RESPONSES
Inability to accept what can't be changed.	Acceptance.
Pessimistic outlook.	Awareness of possibilities.
Negative self-image.	Detachment from self-talk.
Unrealistic expectations.	Detachment from role or peer pressures.

GOOD AND BAD STRESS

Moderate amounts of stress at specific times in our lives can be good for us. Stress can activate us, pushing us to rise to challenges and enabling us, in the process, to discover our strengths. It builds resilience. But when the "fight or flight" response is repeatedly or chronically activated, without returning to homeostasis (stable bodily conditions), it leads to more toxic stress that wears us down, narrows our perspective, and overwhelms our inner resources. Mindfulness is the optimum way of dealing with this situation.

anger arising. This can be a prompt for self-examination. Did we really have an emotion surrounding that person, or does the cause of the emotion lie elsewhere, in some past frustration? Once we have identified the true emotion and given it a name, we are no longer angry with our colleague.

Mindful responses to stress

We often react to stress by feeding it with rumination, memories, and emotional logic (valid or otherwise). A mindful response, on the other hand, directs our attention to the raw data of the moment—the fluttering heart or tense muscles—rather than the story we're busy constructing to explain our stress and to decide how we are going to deal with it. Focusing on the body allows the alarm moment to pass more quickly. We don't stay as activated for as long; and so the next trigger doesn't go on to build stress on top of that caused by the last one. We come home to the present, to base camp, better prepared to deal with the next event.

STRESSFUL FEEDBACK

A feedback loop occurs whenever a cause results in an effect that then feeds back to strengthen the cause. This happens with stress: an initial stressor triggers physiological symptoms of stress, continued anxious thinking, and perhaps avoidant or reactive behaviors. Left unchecked, these reactions reinforce the stress (see below). Individual symptoms of stress, such as fatigue and sleeplessness, can also be amplified by their own negative feedback loop. On the following pages you will learn more about applying mindfulness to break such negative cycles.

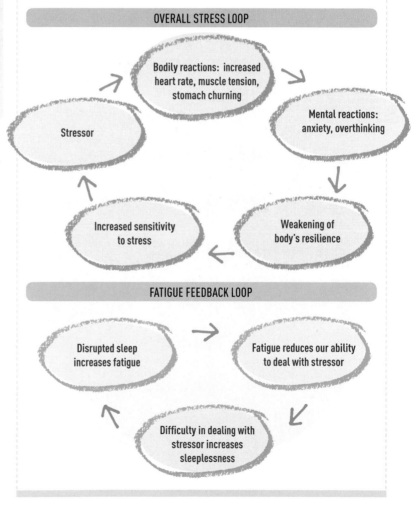

OVERALL STRESS LOOP

Stressor → Bodily reactions: increased heart rate, muscle tension, stomach churning → Mental reactions: anxiety, overthinking → Weakening of body's resilience → Increased sensitivity to stress → Stressor

FATIGUE FEEDBACK LOOP

Disrupted sleep increases fatigue → Fatigue reduces our ability to deal with stressor → Difficulty in dealing with stressor increases sleeplessness → Disrupted sleep increases fatigue

CALM WITHIN
HOW TO UNRAVEL STRESS

Mindfulness tackles stress not by trying to eliminate or fix it. Instead, it enables us to be more aware of the thoughts, feelings, and sensations that keep it going. With the help of this awareness we can open up available possibilities and take action accordingly.

Deadlines, frustrations, and demands can bring high levels of stress into our lives; so can issues stemming from a poor self-image. Either way, stress can soon start to feel as though it's part of our identity. More than feeling merely familiar, it can even seem normal.

However, when stress causes symptoms such as insomnia and an inability to concentrate, you cease to function with full effectiveness. Not only does happiness then begin to seem an impossible dream, but you may have little success in much of what you attempt to do—including keeping your relationships in good shape. And because that makes you feel worse, you get stuck in yet another self-defeating feedback loop (see page 157).

Stress-beating strategies

Understanding your stress is the starting point for dealing with it. You will need to recognize and overturn the tendencies we all have to avoid dealing with issues, such as procrastinating over difficult decisions, or taking refuge in drinking or eating too much. Use the stress map opposite to help you spot the symptoms of stress. It helps if your self-understanding extends to the contribution that family and friends can make. Some people might imagine that calling upon their support network would be a failure of self-reliance. However, this is to underrate the value of empathy: mindfulness practice fine-tunes your relationships, so that when stress strikes you'll have an important source of loving energy to draw upon. Reaching out to others increases your resources, helping to bring matters into balance again.

Other key skills in coping with stress include the ability to calm yourself when emotions surge wildly (see pages 130–31) and to make reasonable assessments of your situation based on the available facts. Understanding how emotions can cloud your judgement by exaggerating some pieces of evidence and suppressing others is part of the self-awareness that is nourished by mindfulness meditation. Emotions can trigger negative thinking (mood-induced cognition), and this just feeds the stress cycle. But mindfully attending to a strong feeling, without falling into the habit of trying to resolve it through thinking or blaming yourself for having unwanted feelings once again, you can starve the cycle of its power.

PRACTICAL STRESS CONTROL

Mindful self-understanding should make it easier for you to adopt some commonsense approaches to reducing the impact of stress in your life:

- Avoid unnecessary stress by saying "no" when you need to, and avoiding people or situations you know will stress you out. Prioritize so that you spend your time in ways you know will be productive, not counterproductive

- Do mindful breath exercises as a quick fix to help you deal with potentially stressful situations (see pages 96–99)

- Exercise regularly. In modern life, where fighting or fleeing are not usually appropriate reactions to threat, aerobic exercise provides a useful surrogate. Take advice from your doctor if you haven't exercised recently or if you have any medical issues. Take long walks often, and use them as an opportunity for mindfulness

- Get enough sleep. Feeling tired can raise stress levels by prompting you to think irrationally. Avoid stimulants before sleep

- Eat healthily. A well-nourished body is better able to cope with stress. Start the day with a wholesome breakfast, cut down on your caffeine and sugar intake, and don't drink to excess.

SELF-MAPPING STRESS

The symptoms of stress are those of common fight or flight reactions: stress can make you feel irritable, aggressive, agitated, or withdrawn. Sometimes it can make you freeze in a kind of emotional paralysis. Recognize and face up to your symptoms with the help of this stress map. Beneath each of the four categories of stress reaction are the helpful attitudes that mindfulness can bring.

RECOGNIZING THE SIGNS OF STRESS

YOUR THOUGHTS
Negative self-talk
Inability to concentrate
Poor judgement
Anxious, racing thoughts
Poor memory

Recognize thoughts as fallible, temporary, and symptomatic.

YOUR BEHAVIOR
Withdrawing from others
Drinking or smoking
Eating too much or too little
Avoiding responsibilities
Nervous habits

Recognize autopilot behaviour as evasive and unhelpful.

YOUR BODY
Aches and pains
Poor digestion
Rapid heartbeat
Loss of sexual desire
Insomnia

Hold these experiences in compassionate attention, allowing them to run their course or to guide you to necessary action.

YOUR EMOTIONS
Feeling overwhelmed
Irritability
Restlessness
Sadness
Loneliness

Create a nonreactive space where emotions can be observed, acknowledged, allowed to rise and fall, and potentially used to generate skillful responses.

AVOIDING AVOIDANCE
HOW TO FACE UP TO YOUR ISSUES

Although mindfulness practice prompts us to see our thoughts and emotions as they really are, and recognize what triggers them, our habitual tendency is to try and distance ourselves from discomfort. Our favorite escape routes tend to fall into two categories: distraction and denial.

Back when humans were hunter-gatherers, running away was a valid response to threat—it was often the only way to survive when an enemy or fierce animal approached. But in today's society, stress—and our reactions to it—usually take more complicated forms. For a start, much of the stress we face is internally caused, perhaps relating to past events, and brought to our attention by physical symptoms such as an aching neck or shoulders. And to complicate matters, we begin to get stressed about our own stress. Our ancient flight reactions don't work against such enemies.

Modern-day flight reactions, though, take creative forms. We might attempt to distract ourselves by a binge of shopping, working out at the gym, movie-going, or doing overtime. Such activities do harm by distorting our values. When work, for example, becomes an escape route, we spend hours doing something not for its own sake but purely as a displacement activity. Our true priorities, such as our relationships, health, parenting, or our friendships, suffer as a result.

Also, of course, we need to recognize a fundamental fact: that escaping a problem leaves that problem unaddressed. The escape can only

STRESS MEDITATION

If you feel you're strong enough to face your true self, you can benefit from building a meditation around one of your stresses. To do this, practice the breath, or body-and-breath, meditations on pages 96–99 and 106–109. When you detect a reaction to stress in your thoughts or emotions, keep your focus on it—transfer it to the laboratory of your mind. You can also choose to summon up a stressful situation deliberately after completing five or ten minutes of breath meditation. Feel free at any point in the following practice to take a step back if you're finding it too disturbing.

1 Be aware of any physical sensations related to the stressful thought or emotion. Hold these in your present-moment awareness with compassion.

2 Focus on your breathing. "Breathe into" the areas of the body where you have the sensations. Welcome the sensations into your open awareness as a key to self-understanding.

3 Turn your attention to your relationship with these sensations. How do you feel about them? Keep your compassion with them, with yourself, and with your acceptance of them, in a triple blessing.

KNOW YOUR ESCAPE ROUTES

Any activity can be entered into mindfully or in a spirit of escapism. Some of the most common avoidance habits are listed below. Be aware of the escape routes that you habitually use, and resolve to stay in the moment to face your issues. Avoiding pain only perpetuates it in the long term, whereas mindfulness lets you learn from and draw strength from your negative emotions.

be temporary: it lasts for as long as the displacement activity, but once we stop and spend time alone again, doing nothing, or trying to function as normal, the problem floods back— often at full strength.

Avoidance and balance

An anxious mind, unconfident in its judgements, can find it difficult to distinguish between activities that are avoidant and those that are part of a balanced life, offering a counterweight to difficulty rather than an escape from it. Mindful self-understanding should clarify the difference. Spending time with friends is not in itself escapist; a sexual relationship may be, if it isn't part of how you see your future.

Confronting issues

It's a key principle of mindfulness that unpleasant and pleasant experiences are treated on equal terms. If you attend to your thoughts and emotions in the present moment, with purposeful awareness, you'll inevitably confront some uncomfortable truths from a safe distance: it isn't that you aren't involved in these truths, only that they have no power over you unless you give them your approval and get drawn into their story. Remember that mindfulness isn't about detachment— it's about engagement.

The important thing is to learn from your mindful encounters with your own experience and to hold any uncomfortable discoveries about yourself in a compassionate embrace of mindful awareness.

Such self-compassion is not a matter of protecting yourself from discomfort, by flight or denial—it's more a matter of being fully aware of your discomfort, seeing how it arose, and recognizing it as an experience from which you can learn and grow.

UNQUIET MIND
HOW TO PUT ANXIETY IN PERSPECTIVE

We all worry at some points in our lives, even though we know that anxiety makes it harder to be happy. But for some anxiety, and the tension it causes in mind and body, persists to the point of interfering with daily life.

Fear is an emotional response to a real threat—for example, being confronted by a mugger, contemplating aging and death, and facing failure will all elicit fear. Anxiety is closely related to fear, and is it caused by stressful situations, which can be real or imagined. If your imagination is vivid, that's a blessing in one way, but it may make your anxieties even more painful.

An anxious type
Many people suffer from a kind of generalized anxiety, which even small issues are likely to set off. How this process works is not completely understood by psychologists, but there seem to be certain factors that can increase our tendency to be anxious. A history of prolonged stress and past traumas seems to be a possible influence. Genetic makeup may also come into play. Another powerful driver is the company of people suggesting, directly or through their behavior, that life abounds in threats or that worry is a useful tool for averting problems. Anxious people also tend to be those with an avoidant coping style—that is, a tendency to steer clear of situations they'd be likely to react to with negative emotions.

Anxiety awareness
As always with emotional reactions, understanding is the first step in learning to dissolve the pattern of harm. Anxiety operates by applying a problem-solving approach to the unknowable future, using a lot of "what if?"questions to trace speculative lines of logic. "What if I miss that train?," "What if I can't afford the rent?," "What if my daughter has an accident?." Sometimes anxiety feeds off itself: "What if I'm so anxious in the meeting that I can't speak my mind?." By "chasing" a worrying thought, we end up entertaining starkly imagined disaster scenarios.

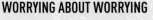

WORRYING ABOUT WORRYING

Anxiety gets bigger when it directs itself inward. Two common false beliefs that can make your worrying worse are:

- My worrying is out of my control
- My worrying will make me ill.

These are negative thoughts that could be self-fulfilling if they are allowed to continue. This is the power of personal myth. But by attending to them with mindfulness, you'll see that you have the option not to be drawn into their gravitational field. As long as you commit to living in the present, these myths will lose their potency.

> Worrying motivates me to get things done.

> But are they the right things, and how well do you do them?

WORRY IS NOT AN ALLY
Anxiety affects us all, so we may try to justify its presence or even adopt it as part of our personality.

At the same time as pursuing unhelpful trains of thought, worriers may avoid confronting their anxieties in the real world. Avoidance, though, only perpetuates anxiety, since it closes off the possibility of it being disproved by a better outcome than was feared.

The part that mindfulness can play in dealing with our anxieties, in addition to building our resilience through meditation, centers around two main approaches. First, it can help us identify the false and unhelpful means we often use to deal with or suppress our worries (see below). Second, by focusing our attention on the present and encouraging us to let go of thinking about the future, it can train us to come to terms with uncertainty (see page 165).

HOW YOU TRY TO CONTROL YOUR ANXIETIES

None of the following strategies is likely to succeed in keeping anxiety at bay. Mindfulness, which involves acceptance rather than control, offers a much more realistic approach.

BOTTLING UP YOUR WORRIES

This is draining, since it takes a great effort of will. It also brings with it an additional worry: the thought that your efforts are not as successful as you need them to be. Moreover, when we conceal our anxieties, we may find ourselves showing various types of compensation behavior, such as passive or aggressive tendencies.

REASONING WITH YOUR WORRIES

This approach fails to recognize that anxiety is an emotion, and not subject to the rules of logical thinking. Reason alone will never win a battle conducted on anxiety's terms.

DISTRACTING YOURSELF

This prolongs the underlying problem, and may lead to extreme behavior—such as excessive drinking—that causes fresh anxiety on its own account.

POSITIVE THINKING

This sounds promising, but again involves engaging in a potentially exhausting battle of attitudes. Positive thinking needs constant effort, and as the default setting, anxiety will win through quite frequently.

STEADY WITHIN

HOW TO DEAL WITH ANXIETY

Anxiety, an emotional reaction to stress, can be so habitual that you start thinking of yourself as *temperamentally* anxious. In your mindfulness practice, attending to the moment-by-moment unfolding of your life, you will begin to see that your "anxious moments" don't have to mean that you're an "anxious person."

A nxiety is a genre of fiction. As a strategy of self-protection that evolved in the early history of humankind to guard us against danger, it exaggerates the reasons for fear, weaving imaginary situations that act like warning notices, deterring us from future mishaps. Reason tells us that living in a state of anxiety is at best nonproductive and at worst harmful to

our mental and physical health, but understanding this is a long way from doing something about it.

Therapy and mindfulness

Over the decades, psychologists have developed a number of therapeutic approaches to deal with anxiety and related problems. One of the most widely used is CBT, or cognitive

behavioral therapy, which works by challenging the content of our self-deceiving negative thinking (see pages 30–31). Mindfulness, however, uses a different strategy: it leaves intact the anxiety-inducing content and encourages us to engage with it differently, with present-moment compassionate awareness. In this way it challenges our *perspective* on anxiety.

POSITIVELY SPEAKING

Some people use the phrase "I'm anxious" to communicate their feelings to others or in self-talk—their internal dialogues.

In saying "I'm anxious," you are identifying yourself with that state, as in "I'm a woman" or "I'm a dentist." In truth, your thoughts and emotions aren't bound up with your identity. Instead, get into the habit of expressing yourself differently: "I'm full of anxious thoughts" is more faithful to the true situation. Beware of using language that perpetuates a negative self-image, identifying yourself with your emotions.

How should I control my anxieties?

You shouldn't. Instead, sit with them and learn from them. Even if they don't go away, at least you won't be spending so much wasteful effort fighting them.

CONTROL FREAK

Anxiety is not the opposite of self-control. It's just another emotion that you can learn from.

It asks us to fully acknowledge the truth—that anxieties are fleeting inner experiences; feeling them is normal and to be expected in life. Accepting this truth is a major step forward in dealing with anxiety; instead of avoiding or withdrawing from anxiety, we stay present with it and fully experience its symptoms. Put another way, rather than running away from distressing thoughts, we open up to them and see how unreliable they are.

When confronting anxieties with mindfulness, you make no effort to avoid or control them. Instead, you respond to them in a way that's in keeping with the situation and with your values and priorities. By taking a bold step toward your anxieties, you enter a new, more constructive relationship with them. You give permission to your anxiety to change in due course into something more rewarding, since you're no longer investing in it.

> **Mindfulness leaves intact anxiety-inducing content and encourages us to treat it with compassionate awareness.**

DEALING WITH UNCERTAINTY

Uncertainty, a characteristic of everyone's life, is handled better by some people than others. Many of us are highly risk-averse, and do anything to avoid situations that have uncertain outcomes. We may even see anxiety as useful, because our worry drives us to play out multiple scenarios in our minds so that no outcome can take us by surprise—we have foreseen the worst that could possibly happen. The diagram below contrasts this delusion with the reality, and then shows how to consider uncertainty with mindful awareness.

THE DELUSION
The worst-case scenario has been foreseen and accepted as a possibility.

THE REALITY
The future is still unknown; and the present is full of anxiety.

Mindfully accept both the delusion and the reality of uncertainty, then consider the following questions:

Is uncertainty a problem for me, given that it's a basic law of the universe? If so, why?

What sensations, thoughts, and emotions do I experience when I notice in myself a need for certainty?

Do I imagine, when the future's uncertain, that bad outcomes are likelier than good outcomes? If so, why?

Can I accept uncertainty on its own terms: I don't know what will happen, and I don't know how I'll respond? If I can't accept this, why not?

WEATHER WARNING
HOW TO UNDERSTAND AND DEAL WITH EMOTIONS

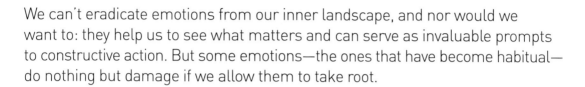

We can't eradicate emotions from our inner landscape, and nor would we want to: they help us to see what matters and can serve as invaluable prompts to constructive action. But some emotions—the ones that have become habitual— do nothing but damage if we allow them to take root.

The idea of emotions as problematic dark forces that we need to either suppress or tame, like a rodeo rider astride a bucking horse, may be apt in a romantic novel, but bears little relation to reality. The truth is that emotions are fleeting—some research suggests that we feel raw emotions for periods of only a few minutes, and some are over in a flash. When emotions do harm it is mostly a result of the way we unwittingly perpetuate them.

The mindful approach to emotions is neither to bottle them up nor to indulge them. There's a middle way of treating emotions with awareness—watching them rise and fall during the storms of stress in which we find ourselves. The more we recognize the temporary nature of our emotions, the less we define ourselves by them and the more we put them in their place. Then, as our mindfulness practice becomes strong, we can begin to explore,

using them to move closer to our inner experiences, finding peace right in the midst of the storm.

Assault course
Each negative emotion has its own way of launching an assault on our calm and well-being. Anger seems to surge from within us, resentment simmers, jealousy makes us feel sick and displaced, fear makes us feel fragile and unstable.

My emotions get the better of me. I don't know whether to keep them in or act them out.

Do neither. Just let them take their course in your body and your mind.

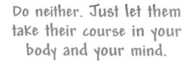

THE MINDFUL ALTERNATIVE
The mindful way is to see the emotion within the broader picture of the life that's going on inside us and outside us. The emotion is tolerated and placed within what in scientific terms might be called a "wider attentional frame"—or in more poetic terms, a "spacious attention."

GAMEPLAN FOR DEALING WITH EMOTIONS

Over the long term, following a program of mindfulness meditation will encourage us not to habitually do battle with our emotions, in an attempt to make them behave better, but to view them as naturally arising reflexes of the body. To approach emotions mindfully as they appear, and to understand your own responses, try applying the four steps outlined below.

1 RECOGNIZE
Name the emotion if possible—is it anger, happiness, loneliness, fear, or jealousy? Or recognize the confusion when lots of emotions are mixed up. Naming an emotion is part of the process of being attentive to the emotion itself, rather than to the underlying content. With an emotion named, detached awareness is strengthened and our capacity for disengagement is reinforced.

2 ACCEPT
Give yourself permission to have the emotion. Apply no censorship, no judgement.

3 EXPLORE
Trace the physical effects. Decide how you know, from the symptoms, which emotion you're having.

4 DISENGAGE
Decline to identify yourself with the emotion. Remind yourself that it is something passing through you, not something that's bound up with you. Dissolve the me and the mine. Don't get entangled.

As an emotion starts to manifest, we usually recognize it and then move into thought, using the emotion as a basis for painful narratives. So if we feel angry with someone, we may replay their old offenses in our minds. If we feel fearful, we vividly portray to ourselves, in a reflex of imagination, the worst-case scenario. In our misguided attempts to "deal with" the emotion, we start reliving (rethinking) the situation that caused it, rehearsing its underlying story… and, of course, refueling the emotion over and over again without realizing it. However, if we focus not on the situation but on the feelings, the bodily sensations, that the situation has caused us to experience—such as trembling, blushing, sweating, and stammering—then the emotion will not continue to be fed by thought. It will run its course and leave us, like a breath flowing out of the body. Being mindful allows emotions to form, unfold, and weaken, until they subside in their own natural way.

Once mastered, this way of dealing with emotion marks a major turning point in many people's lives. It often takes a great deal of practice, but when we have learned how not to respond to emotion with thought, it's incredibly liberating. Emotions are experienced more freely, requiring less energy; and in their "pure" form (not exaggerated or reshaped by the narratives they evoke) they can be used to really guide us to ascertain what's called for in each moment of our lives.

SHIFT WORK
HOW TO DEAL WITH CHANGE

Whether we seek out change in our lives, or have it imposed on us by external forces, it can take mental strength and flexibility to adapt to new circumstances. Mindfulness paves the way by encouraging us to confront rather than suppress our difficulties.

Notches on the door frame marking a child's growth remind us that life *is* change. Failing powers in older family members may also prompt us to reflect. Yet our own aging tends to proceed by stealth, too slowly for us to be aware of it. And our home and work lives (kids aside) can acquire an apparent permanence, reflecting choices we've made in the past. It's when we seem to be settled and happy that big changes beyond our control—from job loss to storm damage—send shock waves through our lives. And these are also the circumstances when we're likely to miss opportunities for *positive* change, because we've become habituated to the status quo.

The art of adjustment
When major surprises happen, dealing with them is a process with many stages—a little like cooking a complicated meal. Applying mindful awareness to any changes in your life as they occur, tuning in to evolving situations around you, and to any changes within your own mind and body, prepare you for the unexpected. Mindfulness also primes you to be flexible enough to adjust to change, while accepting the thoughts and emotions change brings in its wake.

When difficult change occurs, it's natural to feel sad, to grieve, to be angry, and to look for something or someone to blame. Mindful meditation will help you recognize these responses without being drawn into them, and will

THE CHANGE EXPERIENCE

The American psychiatrist Elizabeth Kübler-Ross (1926–2004) described a seven-stage cycle of experience people go through in grieving. We have similar experiences when we deal with other big life changes. Emotions, such as blame, anger, and frustration, will most commonly occur in the shock, denial, and discontent stages, but may resurface in recovery stages too. Attend with mindfulness to emotions and negative thoughts to ease your way through your transition.

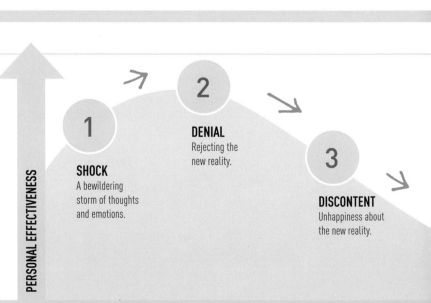

PERSONAL EFFECTIVENESS

1
SHOCK
A bewildering storm of thoughts and emotions.

2
DENIAL
Rejecting the new reality.

3
DISCONTENT
Unhappiness about the new reality.

TIME

FIVE-POINT PLAN FOR CHANGE

Mindfulness makes you better equipped to accept and adapt your thinking to change. Here are some specific action points:

- **Keep up your mindfulness meditations**. If you've allowed them to lapse, restart a daily routine

- **Acknowledge your thoughts and emotions** with mindful compassion

- **Give yourself time to adjust**—set your own pace, whatever others tell you

- **Stay true to your priorities and values**: don't forget the things that haven't changed

- **Communicate**—draw strength from others when it's available.

open your mind to the options you have available—the pathways leading from this moment to a life of your choosing.

Protecting your self-image

Many people, going through stressful change, feel pressure to project to others and to themselves an image of being strong and unafraid, disguising how vulnerable they really feel. This might result in their failing to seek help from others when they most need support. Mindfulness not only tells you that vulnerability is acceptable, but also shows that any reluctance to call upon friends and family for help stems from a kind of pride. If you do appeal to others,

pride can also work against you by deterring you from telling them precisely how they can help.

Human ability to adapt to new circumstances is truly astonishing; those people who find themselves unable to adapt to change have usually convinced themselves that it isn't possible. Mindfulness can help here too, by defusing the power of negative self-talk, such as "I can't learn a new way to do this," or "I'm too old to change my habits," discouraging us from clinging to the past. Change gives us a great opportunity for learning about ourselves, and in the process we grow stronger as well as wiser.

> # Mindfulness primes you to accept the thoughts and emotions that change brings in its wake.

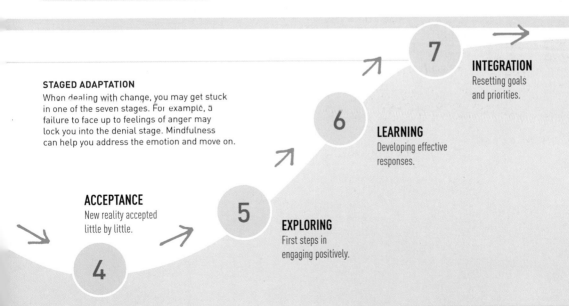

STAGED ADAPTATION
When dealing with change, you may get stuck in one of the seven stages. For example, a failure to face up to feelings of anger may lock you into the denial stage. Mindfulness can help you address the emotion and move on.

7 INTEGRATION
Resetting goals and priorities.

6 LEARNING
Developing effective responses.

ACCEPTANCE
New reality accepted little by little.

5 EXPLORING
First steps in engaging positively.

4

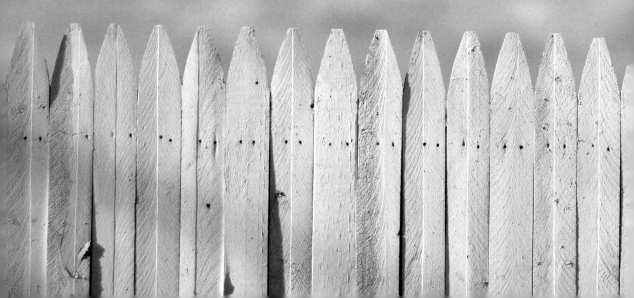

"Learn to wish that
everything should come to
pass exactly as it does."

Epictetus (*c*.55–*c*.135)

AWAY WITH AUTOPILOT!
HOW TO REINVENT YOURSELF

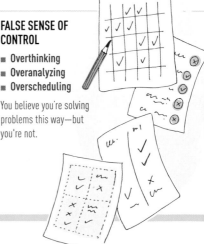

Reinventing yourself may sound like a gargantuan task, but mindfulness teaches that behaviors and thoughts which you believe to be fixed actually depend on your permission. Opt mindfully for your true priorities in life and habits will lose their power.

In autopilot mode our habits make our choices for us. Habitual tendencies, cravings and aversions, preferences and prejudices, look like fixities: over time they've become seemingly impossible to shift. These habits set up invisible walls around us that restrict our freedom and prevent us from attaining our full potential for happiness.

This can happen in any area of life—a relationship might be damaged by our inability to let go of some long-held grievance; or we might struggle in vain to keep our weight down or stop overspending. All this is down to the power of habit, driven by repetition, until it becomes part of our lives.

Resolution and intention
Forming a resolution, often around New Year's Day, is the time-honored approach to breaking habits, but this seldom brings lasting results. A resolution is a statement of firm intention, but it isn't backed up by real power. It's like using a sieve to dam a stream: it's the wrong tool for change.

FOCUS ON FALSENESS

To be mindful is to be truthful about yourself—to see things as they are and to acknowledge that perception. Directing awareness to the delusions inherent in your habits (see right) will rob them in the end of their compulsive power. You'll then explode a further delusion: that your habits are yours forever.

FALSE COMFORT IN EXCESS
- Food
- Drink
- TV
- Sleeping
- Shopping

These pursuits are neutral in themselves, but can turn into addictions.

FALSE SENSE OF CONTROL
- Overthinking
- Overanalyzing
- Overscheduling

You believe you're solving problems this way—but you're not.

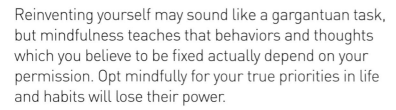

BREAKING THE HABIT CYCLE

The diagram below shows the consequences of being led by our bad habits—avoidance and stagnation. Mindfulness is the key to transforming unproductive, harmful habits into healthy, rewarding behaviors. With self-awareness, in the moment, we can take responsibility for ourselves and make long-term changes that improve our chances of well-being and happiness.

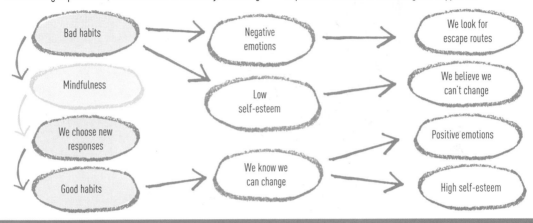

At best it tends to buy a period of reprieve. To deal with habits effectively, we need to delve much deeper into ourselves, in mindful awareness, and form deeply felt intentions.

The patterns formed by your habits are not usually difficult to discern, though the experience can be uncomfortable. Unless you attend to this self-examination with mindfulness, you're likely to shy away from your discoveries. Bringing compassionate acceptance to your habitual reactions to particular triggers, and to the usual consequences of those reactions, is the basis for change. A key role in the process is played by your intuition, which, when it operates mindfully in the moment, is wiser than your autopilot. It will help you recognize your habitual pattern, and tell you how it's harmful. Trust your intuition to alert you to your true priorities and the choices you need to make to be faithful to them.

Mindful transformation

Through mindfulness, you progressively bring everything under the umbrella of conscious awareness. Any action you take needs your acknowledgment and permission. There's a space in the mind where you're free to make your choices. Mindfulness takes you into this space and gives you the power to do things differently.

FALSE SENSE OF AVOIDANCE

- **Procrastinating**
- **Saying "yes" when you mean "no"**

You put off confrontation—but this only causes anxiety because you know you will have to face the inevitable.

FALSE SENSE OF EVADING RESPONSIBILITY

- **Lack of punctuality**
- **Letting people down**
- **Saying "just this once"**
- **Lying**
- **Gossiping**

You fail to take account of inevitable consequences.

I CAN, I DESERVE

HOW TO BUILD YOUR CONFIDENCE AND SELF-ESTEEM

Doubts about our own worth and competence can build up over time into a powerful myth that blocks our path to happiness. A mindful approach helps us dissolve our negative self-talk and enter a virtuous cycle of growing self-esteem.

When your self-esteem is low, your thought patterns are charged with discouragement. These patterns become habitual, carrying messages of self-doubt and criticism—you're too timid, too stupid, too clumsy, or too fat. And even if you receive positive messages from within, or from other people, chances are that they'll be drowned out by these nagging negative voices. When you doubt your own abilities and worth, you cannot fully trust your own thoughts and judgements about yourself. So how can you emerge from such a negative cycle of thinking?

This is where mindfulness can help. When you observe your thoughts with mindful, nonjudgemental awareness in the present moment, you can see when they aren't serving you well. Mindfulness slows down your habitual thinking patterns by encouraging you to stop and observe them.

Recognizing low self-esteem

Self-doubt and low self-worth can creep subtly into your life in many ways; the sooner you realize, the sooner you can act mindfully to prevent negative habits forming.

Do you feel at fault when hoped-for things don't happen? For example, if a friend doesn't call for a few days, do you simply think she's busy, or wonder what you've done to upset her? If you blame yourself, this indicates low self-esteem.

Do you function perfectly well among friends and family only to lose confidence in situations where you're being judged (for example, in an interview) or where you *feel* you're being judged (for example, at a party)? If this happens to you habitually, it could point to a problem with self-worth. Mindfulness can help you overcome such short-term confidence lapses, so that you don't become avoidant— perhaps steering clear of situations where you know you'll feel vulnerable.

Building blocks

Self-confidence affects the way we feel about ourselves, the way we are with other people, and our ability to relax. It increases our chances of happiness by making it easier for us to realize more of our potential. Believing in ourselves and feeling confident enough not to be deterred from worthwhile efforts because we're too afraid of failure are key attributes that mindfulness supports by stopping our ears to the siren song of negative self-talk.

> Self-doubt and low self-worth can creep subtly into your life.

SIX-POINT PLAN FOR CONFIDENT LIVING

If you are held back by a lack of self-belief reinforced by negative self-talk, try following this six-point plan to boost your confidence.

1 **Accept your mistakes** with self-compassion
2 **When facing a challenge** don't indulge in unhelpful worries about your abilities
3 **See the fuel of success** as your pure intention—not as your wish to overwrite your record of past failures
4 **Be yourself**—mindfulness shows you who you are and how to find and follow the opportunities open to you
5 **Do plenty of what you're good at**—even if others don't see it or understand it
6 **Make a contribution**—knowing you've made a difference will boost your self-esteem.

THE VIRTUOUS CYCLE OF SELF-ESTEEM

In the vicious cycle of low self-esteem, self-doubt causes you to lower your goals and fall short of achieving them—which only makes you doubt yourself more. Anxiety plays a part too by muddying your focus. Through mindfulness, you can throw off the undermining influence of low expectation and keep yourself separate from your performance worries. Success—even if it's limited to knowing that you did your best—builds your confidence, and starts a new virtuous cycle of personal growth.

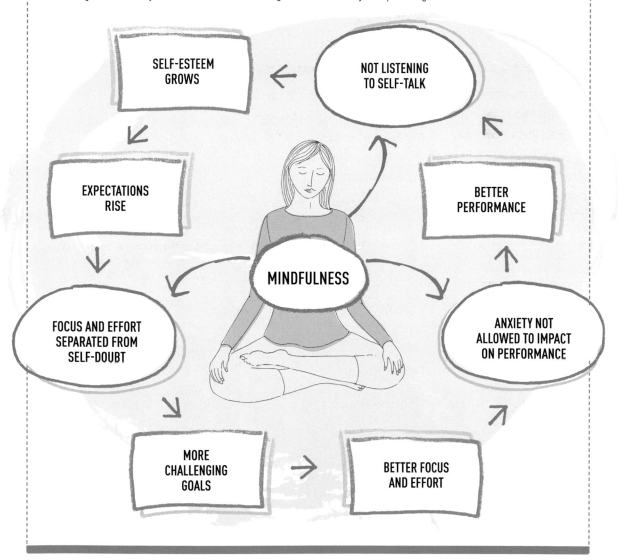

SELF-ESTEEM GROWS

NOT LISTENING TO SELF-TALK

EXPECTATIONS RISE

BETTER PERFORMANCE

MINDFULNESS

FOCUS AND EFFORT SEPARATED FROM SELF-DOUBT

ANXIETY NOT ALLOWED TO IMPACT ON PERFORMANCE

MORE CHALLENGING GOALS

BETTER FOCUS AND EFFORT

WITHIN SEVEN BREATHS

HOW TO MAKE DECISIONS

Decision-making is partly intuitive, partly rational. Emotion might creep in and distort our judgement—anxiety, for example, might make us prevaricate—or our choices might be colored by what other people think of us. Mindfulness, by honing our thoughts and our focus, offers a way to avoid such pitfalls.

We think, we decide, and then, with deliberate intention, we act. Some people are naturally decisive, while others are prone to sway this way and that before taking the plunge. But even the most decisive types might find, when confronted by complicated circumstances, that they need extra time to come up with a course of action they feel confident about.

In medieval Japan, a samurai warrior was expected to make a decision within the course of seven breaths. Sometimes, in our modern world, that will be possible, even easy, but our first thoughts are not necessarily our best. Big decisions, for example about moving house or changing your job, benefit from analysis and reflection.

Challenge and complexity

Emotions can affect decision-making both ways. You might look favorably upon one opportunity because you

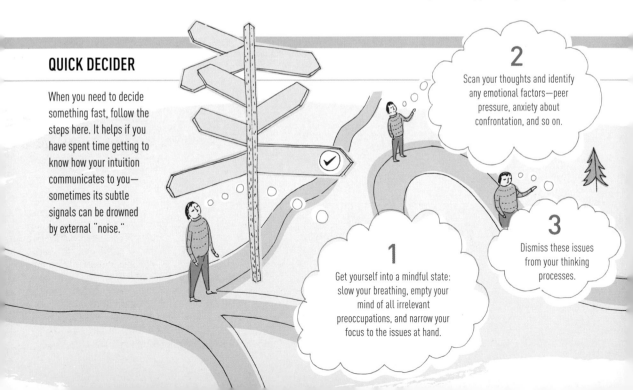

QUICK DECIDER

When you need to decide something fast, follow the steps here. It helps if you have spent time getting to know how your intuition communicates to you—sometimes its subtle signals can be drowned by external "noise."

1
Get yourself into a mindful state: slow your breathing, empty your mind of all irrelevant preoccupations, and narrow your focus to the issues at hand.

2
Scan your thoughts and identify any emotional factors—peer pressure, anxiety about confrontation, and so on.

3
Dismiss these issues from your thinking processes.

feel warmly about the person offering it to you; or you might turn down another chance because you'd need to step too far outside your comfort zone.

We tend to get conflicted about challenges. On the one hand, we may relish the prospect of stretching ourselves and even earning acclaim for achievement; and on the other hand, we may doubt our abilities and fear making fools of ourselves. Mindful meditations, by banishing needless worries and strengthening our self-esteem, can defuse the emotional charge surrounding a challenge and enable us to accept it more straigthtforwardly. "Perhaps I'll succeed, perhaps I won't; but why not give it a try?".

Double anxiety

When making decisions, many of us find ourselves caught in a double anxiety: we worry, not only about the negative sides of the options available,

but also about whether we're making the *right* decision. The stress caused by this uncertainty can continue long after the action has been taken, transforming itself into a question to which there's often no answer: "If I'd done B, rather than A, would that have been better?".

Mindfulness doesn't concern itself with hypothetical situations and so can cut through much of the fog that surrounds decision-making. As you become more grounded and self-aware, you'll accept that the past can't be reversed. Even definite regretfulness is a pointless waste of mental energy; worries about not knowing whether you *ought* to be regretful are doubly so.

> Mindfulness helps you differentiate intuitive from reactive responses.

HOW MINDFULNESS IMPROVES YOUR DECISION-MAKING

Mindfulness helps you make better decisions in life because it:

- Reduces stress, which interferes with clear thinking

- Makes it easier for you to concentrate on essentials

- Makes it less likely that you will get distracted

- Helps you filter out mental chatter

- Liberates you from past patterns of behavior

- Raises your self-esteem, so your choices are more confident

- Helps you resist the pull of emotions.

4 Engage with the logic of the situation in a neutral fashion and weigh your options carefully.

5 Ask yourself what your intuition is telling you to do. Attend to the twitching of its internal antennae—does it confirm your rational judgement? If not, do you know why it's sending you a different message?

6 Clear a space in your head for your final choice among alternatives.

7 Make the choice cleanly and decisively, without regretful backward looks.

CLEAR THINKING
HOW TO RECOGNIZE EMOTIONAL BIAS

Our minds are wonderful tools, but they are subject to biases of all kinds—usually resulting from the influence of our emotions. We may think we're being logical, and might use words like "because" and "therefore" to describe our thought processes, but emotions can stage a coup, to rule our decisions in place of intellect.

An untrained mind, with no meditation experience, will tend to be more reactive in its decisions, allowing previous patterns of experience to repeat themselves.

A classic example is the person who chooses the same type of partner each time, despite a track record of breakups; or someone who delays giving up a bad habit, deciding that one final indulgence will be the last. The mindful approach is to look at each decision in the light of your priorities and values, which often means taking the longer view and making short-term sacrifices.

DISTORTED THINKING

When our thoughts are selfishly calculating, we're usually damaged in the end—not only morally. Emotional bias can distort our ability to achieve a good outcome for ourselves. This becomes evident in the "ultimatum game"—a scenario played out by theoretical economists. Imagine someone gives you $100 on the condition that you share it with your acquaintance, Mary. You can offer Mary as much or as little as you want, but if she rejects your offer, neither of you keep any of the money. Mary knows the rules of the game too. Logic dictates that you offer Mary as little as possible—say $1; and logic suggests that she accepts. After all, $1 is better than nothing. But with this game, the outcomes are usually very different.

I want to keep as much cash as I can for myself.

I'm expecting a fair offer.

When considering mindfulness in decision-making, it's important to draw a distinction between living *in* the moment and living *for* the moment. To say to yourself, "Never mind the consequences, I want this now and I'll take it," is far from mindful. Full awareness is not a pair of blinders: the whole point of mindfulness is to broaden your perspective rather than narrow it.

> Taking your focus away from what happened in the past and what might happen in the future helps you take better decisions now.

REDUCING BIAS IN IMPORTANT DECISIONS

Enhanced awareness of the present moment offers an antidote to many errors in decision-making. One common error, called "sunk-cost bias," is our tendency to carry on down a path once we have already invested time, money, or effort in that direction. The phrase comes from the world of business, but we often show sunk-cost bias in our daily lives too—just look at the examples below. Research carried out at one of the world's foremost business schools, INSEAD, has shown that brief sessions of mindfulness meditation greatly reduce vulnerability to this form of bias.

- **I've invested in a relationship,** but have found we have irreconcilable differences. Instead of breaking up, and starting afresh in our search for emotional happiness, we struggle on.

- **I've invested in a career with a company,** and I'm uniquely expert in the way they work, but there is no scope for promotion. Instead of wasting all my knowledge and skills, and moving on to something new, unhappily I stay.

- **I've paid for tickets** to a music festival, but my partner has the flu and the weather looks threatening. Instead of writing off the cost of the ticket, we go anyway, because not to do so would be a waste of hard-earned cash. We end up having a cold, miserable time—and both come back ill.

EMPATHY
HOW TO TUNE IN TO OTHERS

> "If you want others to be happy, practice compassion. If you want to be happy, practice compassion."
>
> His Holiness the 14th Dalai Lama

Our connections with others, strengthened and enriched by mindfulness, provide us with a major source of happiness. A large part of this comes from giving—not just our warm and loving feelings but also, when needed, our practical compassion.

We can't read other people's thoughts, and nor can others read ours. Why, then, don't we all feel completely alone? The answer is that we deliberately form deep connections in our relationships. Getting to know someone starts with simply exchanging information, but this often develops into profound fellow feeling, a sense of affinity even when you're physically apart. This intuitive understanding of other people is empathy—what makes us appreciate, forgive, and feel warm toward others because we partake of their emotional lives. Empathy is a close relative of two other graces: sympathy and compassion.

The mindful connection
Research has shown that meditation activates the part of the brain known as the insula, which seems to play a key role in our empathy for others (see pages 110–11). In accord with these findings, self-assessment studies undertaken on regular meditators have suggested that meditation increases our capacity for empathy and allows empathy to extend beyond the circle of

our acquaintance to embrace people in general. This enriches our relationships and our ability to communicate.

Mindfulness meditation starts with the self, the center of all our connections, and asks initially that we direct compassion inward, in the present moment, toward our own thoughts and emotions. We may be

tempted to engage with them, but instead, since our choice is to be mindful, we simply acknowledge them with affection, like a parent cuddling a child. In the process of self-discovery we become more grounded and at the same time our awareness is expanded. It's as if, in directing our powers of empathy into a big jar inside ourselves, it fills to the brim and starts overflowing for the benefit of others.

Giving more
As we continue our practice and turn away from exhausting inner battles against negative thoughts and needy emotions, we find ourselves able to give

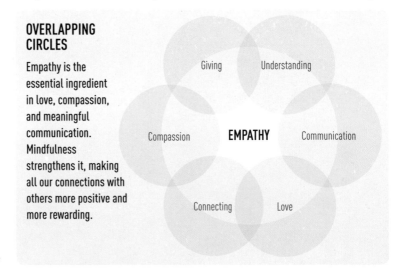

OVERLAPPING CIRCLES

Empathy is the essential ingredient in love, compassion, and meaningful communication. Mindfulness strengthens it, making all our connections with others more positive and more rewarding.

Giving Understanding

Compassion **EMPATHY** Communication

Connecting Love

DEVELOPING EMPATHY

We are all empathic to some degree: humans evolved in social groups where empathy was an adaptive advantage. Some of us have deep wells of empathy, able to intuit the feelings of others, while others can become more empathic through mindfulness practice.

Some psychologists believe that our natural reserves of empathy depend on the closeness of key relationships within the first few years of our lives. Here are five simple, practical steps you can take to build empathy into your everyday life.

2
BE OPEN
Prejudice is a block to understanding. Examine your preconceptions about people and put them aside when you talk to them.

3
LISTEN
Really listen to what others say, and try to understand their emotional state and needs.

4
BE CURIOUS
Talk to people when you don't have to—fellow passengers on the bus, the barista, the store assistant. Inquire gently about their lives.

1
DO SOMETHING DIFFERENT
Try doing things that you've seen others doing, but never tried. Put yourself in some else's shoes for a while.

5
DO SOMETHING GOOD
Make a commitment to help someone who needs help. See this commitment through.

more. Also, since we've started to think of ourselves *without judgement* (to use that key phrase in the definition of mindfulness), we're primed to extend this tolerance to others. Our enhanced understanding makes us more acutely aware of our values, and given that our empathy is awakened, this is likely to include the importance of others. Like us, many of our fellow humans are doing their best to overcome their limitations, set their true priorities, and

find their own version of happiness. In place of disappointment, forgiveness becomes our natural response.

Practical empathy
Empathy directed at a person in distress is not a comfortable experience, since it's to feel something of what the other is feeling, by projecting yourself into their being. However, it is far from mindful to turn your back on reality just because you find it too upsetting.

Mindful self-understanding makes you more aware of any suffering, without getting so absorbed in it that your power to help is weakened. That's when compassion comes in. Compassion could be defined as the executive arm of empathy, based on fellow feeling but flowing from a wellspring of strength, since in your mindfulness you know you must be strong enough to satisfy your urgent priority—to give the warmth and support you feel is needed.

THE MINDFUL CONNECTION

HOW TO ENHANCE YOUR RELATIONSHIPS

You might spend time with certain people out of habit or because your family or social circle expects it. Although mindfulness dissolves patterns of habit, that doesn't necessarily result in your breaking off such connections. Better to look again mindfully at the relationship, and see if you're contributing to its imperfections.

PRACTICE LOVING KINDNESS
The loving kindness meditation, described on pages 138–41, is a healing way to think with warmth and compassion of others—not only those close to you, but also distant acquaintances. Build it into your regular meditation routine, making time for it at least once a week.

Every relationship you have has the potential to enrich your life. True, some people put up walls that limit their openness, or have completely different approaches to life that you may find unacceptable, but it's always worth asking yourself some probing questions. Are those walls as much of your making as of theirs? Isn't difference attractive, for its fresh perspective, rather than a reason for you to back off from a relationship? What are the true sources of the discomfort you feel with this person? Mindfulness is capable of providing helpful answers to these questions.

First impressions
It's easy to make snap judgements about people based on factors such as their appearance, their job, their friends, or other scraps of information. Many people do indeed form lasting opinions about others based on a short first meeting. However, if you can summon up true awareness, you'll see that first impressions are a flimsy basis on which to build firm conclusions.

Cultivating connections
Expanding your awareness to others, and the possibilities for connection, will start to make you more open-hearted. You'll see how far a smile can take you, or a joke, or a pleasant "Good morning" greeting. Any act of thoughtfulness or kindness, from either side, is likely to make a relationship warmer. Mindfulness, by clarifying

BE FORGIVING
Be watchful for any signs of resentment in yourself: ask yourself what's preventing you from forgiving. People may have wronged you in the past, but focus on the present, and give them the chance to come back into your life in a renewed relationship.

the choices you make, will help you avoid pigeonholing people and the kinds of relationships that are appropriate for you to have with them. You'll see through cultural clichés and discover your own way of moving toward a life-enhancing closeness.

PRACTICE PRACTICAL COMPASSION

Look for ways to convert your empathy for others into practical acts of compassion. Be open-hearted to your workmates and neighbors as well as people closer to you. Think about the needs of other people and how you can help to meet them.

A true connection with someone is a vital experience that you feel in your whole being.

COMMUNICATE WITH AWARENESS

Be open and flexible in your communication. If you see habitual patterns developing, step aside and choose another way. Tune in attentively, not only to the words but also to any unspoken messages, and respond with good-hearted intention. Use touch where appropriate as well as warm words. Walls of separation will then start to dissolve.

FIVE-POINT PLAN FOR MORE REWARDING RELATIONSHIPS

STEP BACK FROM CONFLICT

During a disagreement, if you sense any annoyance or frustration in yourself, pause to pay mindful attention to your emotions. To step back from conflict is to offer yourself and the other person the gift of preventive relationship medicine. Don't let your sense of being right derail you.

MAP AND QUESTION

Sketch a map of your most important relationships, using overlapping circles to indicate the degree of closeness. Choose ten people among family and friends. Ask yourself:

Write down the answers, and think about how you can use them to enrich the relationships. Make an action plan to make the "kind thing" happen for each relationship.

- How do I nourish these relationships?

- What would I like to change in them?

- What can I do to bring about these changes?

- For each one, is there one kind thing I can do now as a gesture of commitment and love?

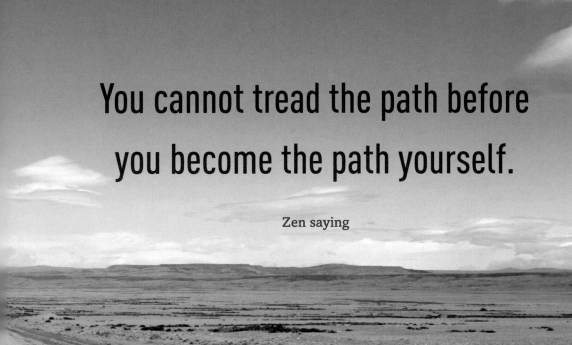

You cannot tread the path before you become the path yourself.

Zen saying

THE MINDFUL COUPLE
KEEPING A RELATIONSHIP ON COURSE

In a long-standing relationship, familiarity can become a breeding ground for habitual patterns of thought and reaction. Certain issues are likely to recur. When automatic reactions set in, you might both become tense and quarrelsome. Keeping a relationship vital and loving requires openness, truth, and commitment.

In the familiarity of a loving partnership, we often find ourselves lashing out—as if the censor that normally inhibits us from expressing certain emotions were suddenly disengaged. Sometimes our closest relationship feels like our most challenging. Romantic relationships bring us happiness but they also test us. In part this is because we can become dependent on the partner's continuing love, kindness, patience—or whatever qualities we've come to expect or hope for in them. Fear of being hurt can make us edgier, more reactive—and put us at risk of sabotaging what we hold dear.

By helping us to become calmer and more centered, mindfulness can act as a useful brake on autopilot reactions that all too quickly can lead to a quarrel. It can defuse defensive responses, by prompting us to question over-hasty assumptions that may spring from our own insecurity.

A RELATIONSHIP CHARTER

Following the guidance here will help your relationship stay on course. Some points relate to potential tensions, others to making the bond even richer.

ACCEPT CHANGE

Don't imagine that your partner should remain as he or she was when you met: like you, they have changed. Don't hanker after the person they once were. They still are that person, but they're in a different place now.

BE AUTHENTIC

Mindfulness trains you in authenticity. Your relationship doesn't need conform to standard templates of behavior, so long as it's rooted in loving kindness. Allow your partnership to be unconventional by setting aside your preconceptions of how a couple "should" be.

REASON APPROPRIATELY

When your partner shows emotions, don't try to present a reasonable case to show that they're irrational. Empathize. Explore these emotions together. Ask sensitive questions to help you both understand them better.

BE AN EQUAL, NOT AN AUTHORITY

Don't imagine that your mindfulness, or any other quality you recognize in yourself, entitles you to wield moral authority over your partner. Turn your back on exerting power—even if it's arguably for the good. Be an ally, not a leader.

People living together tend to store up grievances unconsciously, and when disagreement hits a flashpoint these past hurts come to the surface, raising the temperature. If this sounds like a cliché, it's one with a sound core of psychological truth. The habit of mindfulness minimizes such wasteful attrition, especially when complemented by shared mindfulness practices, involving eye gazing or touching (see right). It's also valuable to engage consciously in mindful communication: you could set specific occasions for this, or resolve, even mid-discussion, that henceforth mindful principles of nonjudgemental awareness will be followed, each communicating calmly and clearly and listening attentively.

Mindfulness can create a space in which a loving bond can flourish. As we become individually more self-aware, our relationships strengthen. In particular, couples who are good at handling stress together tend to have stable bonds.

LEARN FROM FEEDBACK

Stop yourself from being defensive when your partner tells you honestly how they feel. Pause and absorb the message they're giving. Ask yourself what's the most positive and loving way to respond. Thank your partner for their honesty.

TRY NEW THINGS TOGETHER

However much you follow your individual pursuits, make time for sharing new experiences. When you do try new things separately, always talk about them, and make plans to do them together next time if one of you found them enjoyable.

EYE TO EYE

Some mindfulness trainers, working with couples, direct them in what are called "dyadic" exercises—a scientific term for interactions within a pair. Try the eye-gazing exercise described below to promote mutual acceptance and closeness. Use a timer, if you wish, to help you move through the stages of the exercise.

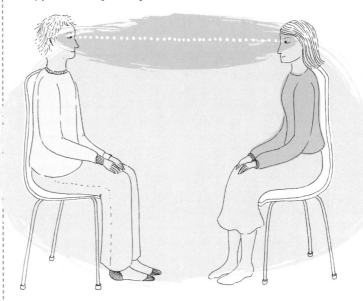

1 Both you and your partner sit upright, facing one another. Arrange your seating positions so that your faces are about three feet apart.

2 Look intently at (rather than into) each other's eyes, and accept without acting upon it any feeling of unease or vulnerability this causes. Each of you should remain attentive to your individual experience: the point is not to communicate but to observe. Do this for about five minutes.

3 Now, instead of merely looking, both of you gaze into each other's eyes. Imagine that behind the eyes is the person. You are not merely looking, you're connecting. Do this for an additional five minutes or so.

4 Finally, while holding your gaze, think of the goodness of your partner, the qualities you love in them; and at the same time think of your own intrinsic goodness. Spend an additional five minutes appreciating, indeed loving, the mutual love of your partnership.

MINDFULNESS WHEN YOU NEED IT

MINDFULNESS IS AN INVALUABLE TOOL FOR DEALING WITH ALL KINDS OF CHALLENGES, FROM FINDING SUCCESS AT WORK AND PLAY TO DEALING WITH TOUGH TIMES.

GROW AND LEARN
HOW TO STUDY EFFECTIVELY

Learning is one of life's most satisfying activities, but to absorb new skills or knowledge efficiently we need to pay mindful attention to a whole range of potential issues, including self-doubt and poor motivation. Mindfulness makes learning more effective and more rewarding.

LIFELONG LEARNING

Learning is not just something you do when you need a qualification. Mindfulness can help you absorb lessons that enrich your life and contribute to your happiness and the happiness of others. Here are some lessons you can learn with mindfulness:

- How thoughts, emotions, and behavior interact
- How love overcomes insecurity and reservation
- How life is full of wonder and surprise
- How ordinary people are capable of greatness
- How wise children are
- How illusory the concerns of the ego are.

There's more to learning a subject than being conscientious and having a good memory. In formal settings, such as schools, community colleges, and universities, you also need to be able to cope with a range of pressures and stresses. Emotions may come into play in any concentrated learning—including doubts about your ability and your mastery of the syllabus—and you'll need to be able to relate to these calmly, without letting them undermine your performance.

When emotions are not well-managed, thinking and motivation can be impaired, and you'll find it hard to prioritize among competing goals.

Under pressure

When you are studying, the best way to avoid being overwhelmed by any difficulties you may be experiencing is mindfulness—in the form of both regular meditation and everyday attitudes. Whether your challenges relate to self-confidence, the stresses of balancing your learning and your home life, or dealing with the sheer quantity of material you have to absorb, you'll find mindful awareness helpful in keeping your studies on course. The distractions may come from within (your own unresolved issues) or from outside (the lure of unscholarly pleasures). When your friends or your partner

The syllabus is daunting. The sheer volume of material! How on earth will I get through it all?

As you get through your life—one hour, one day at a time.

LEARNING PERSPECTIVE
Mindfulness helps us avoid becoming emotionally overwhelmed by a large program of study.

aren't under the same pressures, the temptation to play hookey is ever present. Such avoidant behavior is the "flight" component in your "fight or flight" response to stress; it offers the path of least resistance but will most likely end in guilt, frustration, and failure. Practicing mindfulness gives you space in which to choose your actions in the light of your true priorities, rather than succumbing to a reflex reaction, and so honor your commitment to learning.

Study flow
When studying goes well, you might enter the "flow state" where you are fully absorbed in your task and lose sense of time passing. Don't forget to be as attentive to the needs of the body as to those of the mind. Do a short breathing meditation from time to time—hourly if possible. Be aware of bodily sensations and act on any warning signs. Get plenty of sleep and eat a balanced diet.

HOW MINDFULNESS HELPS YOU LEARN

There is evidence that mindfulness practice changes how we respond to stress—possibly by affecting how the brain's prefrontal cortex interacts with older brain structures that govern fear and other emotions (see pages 110–11). Educators recognize that such practice also helps to shape a mind that is more prepared for learning, by improving performance in the areas shown below:

WORKING MEMORY
Enables you to hold many separate items of information in the mind, while processing them as a whole.

CONCENTRATION
Enables you to apply yourself to the task at hand, and absorb what you read or hear.

PLANNING
Enables you to map out a sequence of work during any particular study session.

REASONING
Lets you access logic to assess the evidence and draw reasonable conclusions.

PROBLEM SOLVING
Enables you to deal with any contradictions in the material you're studying, and overcome difficulties of comprehension.

MULTITASKING
Balances your learning with other demands and allows better prioritization of tasks.

CONFIDENCE
Boosts your belief in your own ability to master a subject, which feeds into your self-esteem.

MENTAL CLARITY
Enables you to keep emotional issues separate from the task at hand.

MENTAL STAMINA
Allows you to remain engaged with your study for longer periods, keeping boredom at bay.

SHOW WHAT YOU KNOW
HOW TO EXCEL IN EXAMS

Studying can be especially stressful at exam time. Mindfulness can help us deal with the anticipation, the intensity, and the aftermath of exams (worrying about grades) in the most effective way. We probably won't avoid stress altogether, but it's good to know that there are ways of making it tolerable.

An exam hurtles toward you, like an asteroid on impact course. This is the one opportunity you have to gain much-needed grades, and you'll be faced with that test however underprepared, under par, or anxious you feel on the day.

Mindfulness techniques can help you to mitigate exam stress. If you're not doing so already, begin a program of breath and body-and-breath meditation (see pages 96–99 and 106–109) at least two weeks before the first exam, and continue the practice during the exam period itself. A pre-bedtime meditation can help you empty your mind before sleep and ward off insomnia. Never use alcohol to help you sleep.

When you are studying for your exams, and negative thoughts come into your head, simply acknowledge them,

THE 7/11 QUICK FIX

This relaxation breathing exercise can be done anywhere, even after you've taken your place at the your desk. Making the out-breaths last longer than the in-breaths stimulates the body's natural relaxation mechanism.

DO A FEW 7/11S:
- At regular intervals during studying
- Whenever you feel anxious or stressed
- Immediately before you answer an exam question
- Immediately after finishing an exam.

1 2 3 4 5 6 7

Close your eyes and count the seconds silently

1 Breathe in through your nose, for as long as it takes to mentally count to seven.

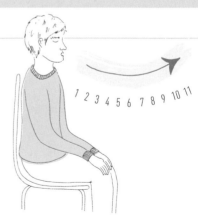

1 2 3 4 5 6 7 8 9 10 11

2 Breathe out through your mouth, for as long as it takes to mentally count to 11.

MINDFULNESS MEDITATION WATCHLIST

When doing the breath or body-and-breath meditation, look out for:

■ Physical symptoms of fatigue. Note them and ask yourself afterward whether you can make any lifestyle changes to help—such as earlier bedtimes

■ Physical symptoms of stress. Note down the symptoms. Do they fade with more meditation?

■ Facts, figures, and ideas drifting into your thoughts. Let them go: save them for your next revision session

■ Self-doubt, which often appears as a thought or a feeling. Just note it and let it go.

give them a name and gently return to the task in hand. Every hour or so, do a 7/11 breathing exercise (see below) and attend to your posture; sitting correctly (see page 94) will help to keep you alert.

If you sit mock exams before the real thing, don't get hung up about the results: that was one test, you now face an entirely different mental tournament. History doesn't have to repeat itself, though it might if you think it will.

Attend to post-exam euphoria mindfully, since it can have damaging effects, even on those normally averse to letting themselves go. The sudden freedom may be tainted by a compulsion to go over your answers and speculate about your grades. Self-worth may be shaken, because—after all—you won't know your worth until you get your grades. Later, too, you may feel you're in a limbo, without purpose. Give yourself time to adjust to normal life again.

MANAGING EXAM TIME

Time management is critical during an exam: you don't want to run short of time to answer questions to your best ability. Here are some tips for managing your exam time wisely.

■ **Practice past papers** while timing yourself. Allot a suitable amount of time (to simulate a real exam) and pace yourself so that you answer all the questions to your best ability before the timer goes off

■ **Now dispense with the timer.** Try another past paper, noting your start time. Don't look at the clock again till you've finished. Keep rehearsing until you've acquired an instinctive sense of the right pacing

■ **Make an affirmation to yourself** before the exam: "I will write the best answers I can within the time available. I will manage the time as needed."

■ **Don't let the subject swallow you up.** Remember: among your possible distractions, one is the subject itself. You're doing an exam, not adding to the sum of human knowledge.

3 Continue this rhythm of breathing and counting for about five minutes, or do just two or three in- and out-breaths when you're pressed for time.

GET THAT JOB
HOW TO SHINE IN AN INTERVIEW

It is unlikely that you'll ever be more intensively or purposefully interrogated, or scrutinized for your personal qualities, than you are in a job interview. Mindfulness offers a way to present yourself more confidently, to say the right things, and to overcome interview nerves.

Sweaty palms, churning stomach, racing heartbeat… then you hear yourself saying things you don't really mean, because your mind isn't in full control of your words. An interview can be grueling. Sometimes it seems like some hideous experiment devised to flush out all your negative thoughts about yourself—your confusions about who you are, what you want, and what you have to give (if anybody's fool enough to accept it). If this is your image of an interview, it could well turn out to be self-fulfilling, since it's the fear of the event, as much as anything, that

IN YOUR ELEMENT: THERE'S NOBODY BETTER

As you walk into the interview room, you are in your element. You've researched the company thoroughly and you know your own résumé backwards, as well as so much that isn't mentioned there. You're the world's greatest expert in the subject you're being examined on—yourself. Nobody could represent you better. This is your comfort zone.

Avoid cliché and jargon—don't spout stock phrases, such as "I'm a people person." Mindfulness involves saying what you mean, in your own way, not imitating what everyone else says.

If you're faced with a panel, **remember they're just a group of individuals** paid to do their job: you're outnumbered but that doesn't make you any weaker.

> Being in the moment helps you focus on the conversation and attend to vital cues that will help you present yourself to best effect.

can sabotage your performance. Behind that fear can be a whole constellation of factors, largely spinning around how badly you expect yourself to perform.

What could go wrong?

If you really want a role, the way you present yourself at the interview may be tinged with desperation. For example, if you dislike your current job, you might unintentionally complain about your employer—this is very common, and never earns you bonus points. Asked about your goals, you might start spouting high-minded nonsense about wanting to make a difference. And quizzed about your weaknesses, you might transparently admit only to the ones you hope will be seen as strengths—such as being too meticulous about detail. If any of these scenarios seem familiar, that might be because you've witnessed yourself performing like this before.

Mindful solutions

Many people fear interviews precisely because they think that they will lapse into a predictable pattern of responses, such as those above.

Mindfulness meditation can help to counter these tendencies by sharpening your focus, strengthening your sense of self-worth, and keeping stress and anxiety at bay. You'll be fully engaged in the conversation, which means that you won't end up saying things that merely sound right. And because you'll be more at ease within your own skin, your personality will shine through—you won't come across as someone who's drilled themselves to give rehearsed answers, but as someone able to engage in genuine dialogue.

Breath meditations

If you aren't already a regular meditator, start with simple breath and breath-and-body meditations (see pages 96–99 and 106–109) as soon as you decide to look for a new job. Aim for at least several weeks of regular practice. Try some 7/11 breathing (see pages 192–93) to calm your nerves while waiting to be summoned. During the interview itself, follow the guidelines below to ensure your performance is as natural and effective as possible, putting all your key skills and qualities on show—not least, mindful self-possession.

Speak at your own pace, in your own tone—the mindful interviewee won't unconsciously imitate the interviewer's manner of speech.

Don't be thrown by surprises, such as personal remarks, an impersonal tone, or a trick question. Be aware of your surprise, or perhaps disappointment, but detach yourself from it. Don't start judging how well or how badly the interview is going.

Let the interviewer lead the dialogue—but answer each question fully, taking care to cover all the relevant points you want to make. Only bring in further points if you can weave them naturally into the conversation.

PAID FOR A PURPOSE
THE MINDFUL WORKPLACE

Work, for the fortunate, means purpose, reward, and the company of congenial and supportive colleagues. But for many, work is associated more with stress, overload, and insecurity. Increasingly, mindfulness is being recognized as the key to making the workplace a happier, more creative, and productive environment.

More and more people are practicing mindfulness at work, often with the encouragement of their bosses. Many high-profile corporations host meditation courses, encourage employees to take paid retreats, or even have an on-site meditation room for their workers.

Studies of such initiatives have reported a whole wealth of benefits, including better communication, more measured reactions to stressful situations, more harmonious teamwork, speedier resolutions to workplace conflicts, and an increase in out-of-the-box thinking. Businesses have reaped the benefits of all this in the form of higher levels of productivity and innovation.

Stress and overload
Stress thrives in the workplace. In industrialized countries, it is second only to musculoskeletal disorders in accounting for the number of working days lost to illness. It is most prevalent in those aged between 35 and 54 who work full-time in jobs such as healthcare, education, and government. Lower-level work stress is arguably

more the norm than the exception—partly because businesses are competitive, and the need to beat the competition can lead to overwork, under-resourcing, and commercial insecurity. Organizations can also generate stress from the sheer

complexity of their functioning. When stress and overwork become endemic, tensions often arise between workmates and it becomes harder for people to realize their full potential.

If work pressures mount we tend to make space for them in our lives by abandoning leisure activities or time shared with family and friends. Narrowing our lives in this way just reinforces stress and fatigue—because the abandoned activities are precisely those that give us vitality. Mindfulness meditations can help to interrupt this downward spiral by helping us see where our best interests lie and acting on those insights—for example, by

GETTING GOOD RESULTS

Participants following a mindfulness program run by a large UK insurance group in 2010 were asked to assess the results, and gave the following feedback:

88% reported "a highly increased ability to stay focused."

76% reported "highly increased positive relationships within their teams."

68% reported "highly increased personal efficiency and productivity."

60% reported "highly increased ability to counteract stress."

CHANGE AT THE TOP

In the late 1990s, business school students were often seen in cafés reading *The Art of War*, a 2,000-year-old classic of military fieldcraft by the Chinese military strategist Sun Tzu. Today their favored reading is more likely to be one of the many mindfulness books by Jon Kabat-Zinn, Mark Williams, or John Teasdale. Mindfulness in business was for a long time associated with Ellen J. Langer, a Harvard psychology professor, who defined it as the "process of actively noticing new things." Increasingly, Kabat-Zinn's MBSR and Williams and Teasdale's MBCT ideas are used in leadership training. One important concept for top business executives is renewal—the use of mindfulness to refresh the self, repairing the damage done by leadership stress.

prioritizing family life over extra work. Workers become much happier and more productive if they can manage their stress, stay objective, be responsive rather than reactive, and show compassion toward themselves and others. Mindfulness training has been proven to help people achieve all these objectives, but it is capable of delivering much more too.

Shed your self-importance, your impatience with tasks you see as beneath you, and your envy of high-flyers. Make yourself people-centered rather than me-centered; notice more and master more details. All this lies within the province of mindfulness. The result will be that work takes on new meaning in your life, contributing more purpose and fulfillment.

POSITIVE DIRECTIONS CHECKLIST

The main proven benefits of mindfulness in the workplace are identified below. You can use the list as a checklist for self-evaluation. Copy it into your journal and measure your progress as you work with mindfulness meditation to meet these objectives.

MINDFULNESS HELPS EMPLOYEES TO:

- ☑ Enjoy their work more
- ☑ Be more flexible in their approach
- ☑ Be aware of more factors relevant to their job
- ☑ Have better relationships with workmates
- ☑ Be more accepting of their role
- ☑ Follow more realistic work goals
- ☑ See problems more as challenges, less as threats
- ☑ Be more considerate to workmates
- ☑ Be less concerned with material reward
- ☑ Be better able to assess their contribution
- ☑ Be more likely to find sources of fulfillment outside work
- ☑ Stay calmer under pressure.

AHEM!
HOW TO MAKE A SPEECH WITH CONFIDENCE

Mindfulness meditation probably won't eliminate your nerves when speaking, but it will give you a positive attitude toward any anxieties that remain. If you build it into your life, and top up with a short breathing exercise before you speak, you have a better chance of being spontaneous, self-possessed, and expressive. You'll reach out to your listeners, within the moment, rather than recoiling from them in fear.

Speaking in public ranks high in the list of people's worst fears. It exposes us to intense scrutiny, which is acutely felt because we are in control of every aspect of our performance. Mindfulness practice can make that thought reassuring, rather than scary.

When you are in the moment you are relaxed, expressive, and spontaneous.

Whenever you address an audience, your goal is to communicate in the moment. If you pay attention to your audience, they will in turn, pay close attention to you. It's very easy, however, to let this dynamic stall. Self-doubt and negative self-talk will make you turn inward, away from the audience, and you'll get distracted if you're continually assessing how well you're doing. If you seize on any perceived signs of boredom in the sea of faces, you'll feel your performance deteriorate. You'll speak the words but not inhabit the words. Such detachment will work against you, since this is a task that requires focus.

Comfort and continuity
To excel at speechmaking, it helps to see it in the context of life as a whole. Work on your anxiety, by accessing, as often as you can, the present moment—the viewpoint from which you see fears as passing experiences that have no bearing on who you are. The most critical thing is focusing on what you're giving and not worrying about what people are taking away.

IDENTIFYING ANXIETY CUES

As with any anxiety, it's helpful to look at your public speaking fears from within the moment, to understand what has triggered them. As you identify each anxiety cue, meet it with a reassuring response to dispel fear and build confidence.

CUE	RESPONSE
It's an unfamiliar venue.	The venue adds novelty to the adventure.
There's a big audience waiting for me.	It's one speech, however many pairs of ears are listening.
There are people listening whose opinions are important.	People will see me as I've chosen to present myself.
The audience is different from me (for example, in gender or background).	I can't second-guess people's prejudices.
I might fluff my words.	If things go wrong, nobody really minds.
People won't like me and they might disagree with me.	I've been asked to speak because I'm qualified to do so.

SIX-POINT PLAN FOR MINDFUL SPEAKING

Over the longer term, mindfulness practice can help you explore what makes you anxious and why, but there are many short-term strategies to reduce anxiety. For example, some people favor breathing exercises or taking a mindful walk before the session. Below are some simple guidelines to help you deliver your best on the big day.

1 PREPARE BOTH CONTENT AND DELIVERY

If you're anxious, you're more likely to find rehearsals stressful and so you may underprepare. Master your script or your notes, allowing ample time for practice.

2 MAKE CONTACT

Before you start speaking, look at the audience and feel a sense of connection. They are playing their part by being quiet and listening. Send them all waves of loving kindness, in gratitude for that. Now play your part.

3 START STRONG

Begin your speech in a firm, confident voice, so negative habits have no space to establish themselves. Starting tentatively in the hope you'll gain in confidence will not work.

4 AVOID THE NOTES/SCRIPT TRAP

If you're working from notes, be sure you know what they mean—your memory might fail. If you improvise around a script, be sure not to get lost. A good approach is to use short notes as prompts for your points, but memorize some key sentences.

5 LEARN FROM "YES, AND"

Improvising actors follow the "yes, and" philosophy, which involves accepting the moment as it is, and adding to it. Instead of stopping the flow, stay with what's happening. Improvise now and then to connect with the audience.

6 USE YOUR BREATH AS AN ANCHOR

Build in plenty of short pauses in which to make contact with the sensations of your breathing. Use this technique to ground yourself. Draw energy up from the ground, imagining it entering your body with your in-breaths.

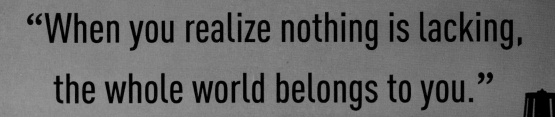

"When you realize nothing is lacking,
the whole world belongs to you."

Lao Tzu (*c.*694–*c.*531BCE)

MINDFULNESS IN MOTION
FITNESS HERE AND NOW

As preparation for sports or other physical activity, regular mindfulness practice is just as important as keeping fit. It trains you to stay focused and motivated, tune in to what your body's telling you (for example, when to stop) and helps to keep any anxieties or frustrations under control.

Whatever your favorite sport or physical pursuit, you will benefit from attending to the messages your body sends you. When you listen to your body, you learn to trust your own sensations and you show self-compassion—a healing kindness toward yourself. Both are important conditions for health and fulfillment.

Before your run, workout, or training session, or after you have warmed up, tune in to these signals and assess what level of exertion your body is ready for.

If, on any particular day, your body tells you that it is tired, or that your quads are sore, listen, and rewrite the script accordingly. Shorten your usual run, take a mindful walk, or simply give your body the rest it needs.

Mindful stretching
Mindful stretching can help to address problem areas, increase your flexibility, and improve range of motion. Bring your attention to the muscle group where you feel the strain. Close

your eyes and take ten slow breaths, directing them, in your imagination, into the muscles concerned.

Sports psychologists know that overthinking exercise can make it seem more exhausting. Mindfulness practice can help here too, because it brings body and mind back together, making them work in harmony. One example here is not to focus on finishing your exercise because that's a kind of craving. Instead, welcome the flow of your fully conscious movements.

THE MINDFUL WORKOUT

Combine mental and physical exercise by staying in the moment during your workouts, and tuning in to your sensations. Focus on your breath and rhythm of movement. Don't distract yourself with music or the TV. Being mindful during a workout can:

- Improve its effectiveness
- Lower the risk of injury
- Increase the pleasure you take in it
- Contribute to a healthy, caring relationship with your body.

Just as mindfulness can improve your physical performance, so exercise can make you more mindful. Studies by German sports scientists of recreational runners found that perceived levels of mindfulness increased greatly over a 12-week training program, in part because the runners became more aware of their sensations—breathing, heart rate, and temperature, and partly because exercise promoted neurological changes that helped the runners stay focused.

MIND OR BODY PAIN? THE RUNNER'S CHOICE

Pain can come from the mind or the body. A runner's pain is often mental—a feeling of frustration at the body's limitations, or impatience at the distance still to be run. Let any thought such as "I can't go on" pass out of your mind, while you focus on your breath and your steps. What is your body saying to you? Do a body scan (see pages 120–25) and ask yourself what's working, and what needs a small adjustment. Set your pace according to what you learn. Stop if your body tells you to, but don't necessarily trust the mind when it's giving you the same message. Follow the key guidelines below to take some of the unnecessary effort out of your running.

Picture a cord through your head, pulling it up toward the sky. Don't slouch your shoulders or stick your head in front of your body. Running tall, with your shoulders over your hips, puts less strain on your body.

Watch and listen to your footsteps, and focus on shortening and silencing your stride. This enables you to cover the same ground with less effort. It reduces bouncing and makes it less likely you'll damage your joints.

Lift your arms high instead of letting them swing from side to side. This makes for quieter landings. And the less you swing sideways, the less tension there'll be on your knees, hips, and back.

PLAYING TO WIN
HOW TO EXCEL AT SPORTS

Different sports make different demands on body and mind—coordination, strength, and stamina to name a few. However, successful sportspeople invariably have one characteristic—mindfulness—although this may be described in traditional terms, such as "being focused," "being in the zone," or having a "winning mindset."

When playing sports there's plenty of space inside our heads for negative "self-talk," which often takes the form of regretting lost opportunities, grumbling about bad play, bad luck, or poor conditions, or thinking that our performance could—and should—have been sharper. Mindfulness meditations can help us dampen such unhelpful mental chatter, providing an antidote to the voice in our heads that says "Useless!," "Loser!," "Give up!"

By mindfully attending to thoughts, we can more promptly notice when a defeatist attitude is setting in, or when distraction or frustration is undermining our focus; and we can then immediately redirect our attention to the moment. Regular meditation can also counter our natural tendency to dwell on errors, replaying them in the mind like video clips. A non-meditator might see losing as a punishment for a weak performance, whereas the mindful way is to accept defeat and move on to the next training session.

Creative visualization
Sports psychologists encourage players to imagine scenes of victory—for example, scoring the winning goal in a game or stepping up on to the podium

WHAT MAKES A GREAT PLAYER?

Many winning attributes in a player's skillset or mindset are positively affected by mindfulness practice. Use the list below to see the influence of mindfulness on these qualities, and learn how it can improve your sports performance.

SKILLS FOR SPORTS	BENEFITS OF MINDFULNESS
Attention.	Helps you enter the flow state.
Focus.	Makes you less susceptible to distraction by pain, thirst, or incidents in play.
Decisiveness.	Helps you make the right play.
Mind-body communication.	Improves speed and accuracy of response.

MINDSET FOR SPORTS	BENEFITS OF MINDFULNESS
Calmness.	Helps you let go of fear and anxiety.
Self-compassion.	Helps you let go of guilt and shame.
Confidence.	Boosts the winner's mentality.
Acceptance.	Lets you cope better with defeat.

OPTIMUM AROUSAL

Sports psychologists plot the mental state of athletes along two axes: engagement (their degree of involvement and commitment) and arousal (the level at which they are attending to and anticipating activity). An athlete who is neither aroused nor engaged is simply bored; and one who is aroused and engaged is excited. Arousal without engagement leads to anxiety, while an athlete who is engaged but not aroused is too relaxed. Competitive athletes aim for a "sweet spot" where arousal and engagement are balanced.

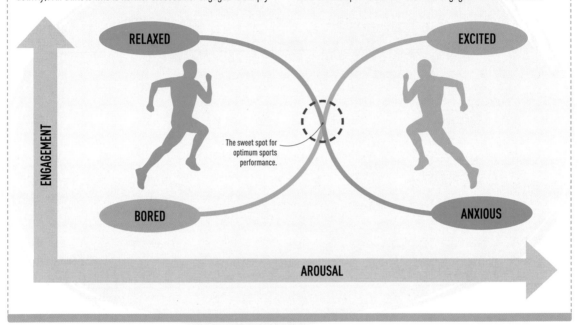

The sweet spot for optimum sports performance.

to accept a gold medal. Such visualization is useful in boosting motivation before an event, but has no place on the field, court, or track, where optimum performance involves total focus, minimal self-judgement, and minimal attention to the outcome

> The mindful way is to accept defeat and move on to the next training session.

of the race or match. Thinking about the medal you're going to win while actually playing is not the way to mindful peak performance—it's a distraction, and will prevent you from entering the flow.

A mindfulness game plan

To improve your performance, try building a program of mindfulness training—such as that outlined below— into your regular training sessions.

Do breath and body scan meditations every day during a training period, and the breath meditation just before you play competitively.

Carry out the stretches suited to your sport, but do so mindfully, noticing the sensations in every muscle.

Do mindful warm-ups—pay attention to what's happening in your body, and to your energy and arousal levels, while loosening up.

Make mindful movements—that is, be mindful when performing the critical actions that characterize your sport, such as serving in tennis or turning at the pool end when swimming.

Extend mindfulness to a complete event—review your progress afterward, and also if there is a break or rest period during a game.

CLINCH THAT DEAL!
HOW TO NEGOTIATE

Hard-bargaining has fallen out of favor in business, replaced by negotiating styles that focus far more on the relationship, creative solutions, and preparing the ground for future cooperation. Mindfulness brings a great deal to the table in making this more enlightened approach more effective.

Negotiations take many forms—from trained, skilled professionals taking part in formal meetings to agree a new contract or an international treaty, to an impromptu bargaining session between friends, for example, over the sale of a car.

In broad terms, you can approach a negotiation with one of two objectives—to achieve maximum gain, or to achieve optimum gain. The first is sometimes called positional or hard-bargaining negotiation; it is often a slightly more sophisticated variation of market haggling. Both sides move from an extreme position toward a mutually acceptable compromise. It's like gambling at cards: success often results from concealing your strength, bluffing, and other ingenious tactics. The aim, for each party, is to make minimum concessions. Today, however, most negotiators across all fields tend to take a longer view of the relationship, and

> The negotiating skills we bring to the boardroom table are similar to those we bring to the kitchen table.

NEGOTIATOR TYPES

What's your natural negotiating style? If you feel you fall into one of the "unmindful" categories below, try to apply mindfulness skills next time you are involved in a negotiation.

MINDFUL NEGOTIATORS HAVE A BROADER FOCUS:

- **Accommodators** relish mutual problem solving. They're intuitively responsive to the subtle signals given out by the person they're negotiating with

- **Collaborators** like tackling difficult problems and finding creative solutions. They have good awareness and good communication skills, and tend to gather detailed knowledge of all the relevant factors.

UNMINDFUL NEGOTIATORS HAVE A NARROWER FOCUS:

- **Avoiders** dislike conflict, and tend to favor email rather than face-to-face negotiation. They often find it hard not to show anxiety and have difficulty defining their goals

- **Competitors** enjoy winning, often using strongly strategic approaches to achieve their goals. They tend not to see "win-win" solutions

- **Compromisers** tend to work to conclude a deal quickly. They're often too ready to make concessions and have no time for the bigger picture.

EXPANDING THE PIE: THE ART OF VALUE NEGOTIATION

Mindfulness equips you with a whole set of skills that are useful in "value negotiation"—the style of negotiation that aims not merely to "divide up the pie" but to "expand the pie:" to release more benefits for all involved. The essential characteristics of value negotiation and the contribution mindfulness makes to them are shown below.

It treats the situation as a shared problem: mindfulness, through compassion, encourages empathy between the parties.

It satisfies the true needs of both parties: mindfulness, by expanding awareness, enables those needs to be accurately identified.

It relies on trust: mindfulness, by encouraging selfless attention, creates an atmosphere where trust flourishes.

It seeks novel, equitable outcomes: by freeing us from past patterns of behavior, mindfulness opens up new ways of thinking.

VALUE NEGOTIATION: WIN-WIN

It uses creativity to gain benefits for both sides: mindfulness, by nourishing intuition, encourages creative solutions.

aim for a "win-win" outcome in which both sides' underlying interests are served as much as possible. This is called "value negotiation" and ideally concludes with both sides feeling respect and trust for one other, and a sense of the negotiation having gone well for them—which makes them likely to want to do business together in the future. Trust, once established, can be a powerful tool in prompting both parties to be open with each other and share information, and this in turn can enrich the possibilities for both sides. Mindfulness, of course, supports the value negotiating style.

Mindful to the room
The most effective negotiating "tactic" is to be mindfully self-aware in the moment, wholly focused on responding to what's said, and alert to everything happening in the room. Emotions are likely to surface from time to time. If you observe signs of them in the person you're engaged with (a nervous laugh, an averted gaze, or a dropped pen), perhaps you should suspect their spoken words. Your own emotions can also be revealing in pointing to unconscious priorities that you can either ignore or act on—while detaching yourself from the emotions themselves and the narratives that come with them. Observing thoughts, emotions, and body sensations in a negotiating session, and yet remaining free from acting upon them, will enable you to conduct yourself skilfully and responsively.

BE HONEST
HOW TO TELL DIFFICULT TRUTHS

How does being mindful translate into your dealings with others? Does it always involve telling the truth? And since mindfulness involves compassion, how should you deal with the truth-teller's conundrum— how to speak a difficult truth with kindness?

Living in the moment when you're with other people is very different to living in the moment in your own company. There's a whole range of transactions going on as thoughts are shared and framed in words, and those words are interpreted and responded to. In addition, there may be a subtle dialogue in body language. To be fully present in such circumstances is to be completely attentive to what's being said, including what you yourself say, and all its implications. It also means being responsive to gestures, smiles, and other signals, whether they are intentional or not.

It isn't always easy to say what you mean, especially when talking about feelings. But mindfulness, as we've discovered, has the potential for enhancing your communication skills, and if you're committed to leading a mindful life you'll often be expressing yourself clearly and openly—while being reserved about what you don't want to say.

Tell or don't tell?
We all keep back information, or opinions, from people if we believe it's appropriate to do so. We're especially guarded when it comes to revealing the truth about ourselves, and today's connected world even has its own term—"oversharing"—to describe being too forthcoming with personal information. Instinctively, most of us avoid the pitfalls of oversharing with strangers, or people who couldn't be described as our intimates. But we might also feel, from time to time, a wish for concealment from people we know really well.

One motive for this could be that you'd promised someone else that you'd keep their secret. But a more common

> ## It isn't always easy to say what you mean, especially when talking about feelings.

Why is being untruthful, by exaggerating, failing to mention something, or telling a downright lie, so harmful to us?

Because it comes out of fear or wanting to be thought well of— and it strengthens the hold these emotions have over us.

HEALING TRUTHS
Telling the truth can be a way of being kind to others and ourselves, but should be done with compassion.

reason for suppressing a truth is the very understandable desire to avoid causing hurt or discomfort—to yourself or to someone else.

The problem with hiding a difficult truth is twofold. First, it brings a negative energy into your relations with both yourself and the person you're concealing something from; if you're mindful, you'll be fully aware of these inner tensions. Second, it is very likely that coming out with your truth will have unpredictable consequences. In particular, you might fear an emotional reaction from the person, but have no idea how strong it will be or what form it will take. You might feel your relationship is too distant for you to be useful as a source of consolation—in which case you might anticipate being embarrassed when the emotion surges

and all you can do is witness it. Or the truth might be so painful that you want to delay its impact for as long as possible, out of kindness. Such thoughts will often be prompted in relation to, for example, news about bereavement or betrayal.

Moments of truth
Biding your time until the right moment is compassionate—as long as that's your real motivation, rather than cowardly procrastination. Mindfulness meditation experience will help you not to panic when the time comes, and not to presumptuously foresee the reaction of the person you're talking to.

All of us are tempted to put the lid on our emotions when we hear disturbing news in front of someone who isn't

either a partner or family. Even close friends, especially when both are male, observe boundaries, and may be reluctant to show signs of being upset in front of one another. Mindfulness often involves understanding and respecting such reticence—yet being compassionate nonetheless, in whatever way you judge would not cause embarrassment. A light touch can say it all.

TRUTH-TELLER'S CHARTER

When you need to break difficult news to someone, don't get so caught up in the difficulty of doing so that you fail to notice any signals given out by the person you're talking to. Be mindful about any emotions you might feel, and detach yourself from them. Consider the following parameters before choosing how to break the news:

- Your relationship with the person
- The moral necessity of telling them this truth
- The importance to their well-being of knowing this truth
- The urgency of their knowing this truth
- The importance of choosing the right occasion to convey this truth.

After considering these points, decide on when and how to speak. Break the news sensitively, responding flexibly to the person's reactions. Remain compassionate and patient even if the truth doesn't go down well.

OFFERING A MINDFUL APOLOGY

One of the principal kinds of truthful speech we're likely to need is apology—being honest, with ourselves and with the other person, about something we've done to hurt or disappoint them. Here are some guidelines for making mindful apologies:

- Confess without omitting anything—otherwise your confession is deceitful
- Don't make excuses, even if they're valid—excuses can creep into an apology, and they always pollute its sincerity
- Let your imperfections be seen—which means lowering your defenses

- Reframe the idea of the apology as a gift that goes both ways. You give the gift of self-revelation by showing your flaws; you receive the gift of authenticity—the other person relates to you as you are—and you might receive the gift of forgiveness.

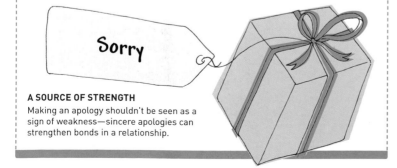

A SOURCE OF STRENGTH
Making an apology shouldn't be seen as a sign of weakness—sincere apologies can strengthen bonds in a relationship.

THEIR TURN
HOW TO GROW MINDFUL CHILDREN

Playing mindfulness games with children and introducing them to simple meditations offers parents and teachers the pleasure of seeing young minds grow in self-awareness—as well as being great fun for all involved. Mindfulness activities like those described here can show kids what it means to have a thought or a feeling and let it go, refocusing on the present.

The ideal time for children to learn mindfulness is at elementary school age, when they are still open to new ways of thinking and are eager to explore their world. They gain a better understanding of themselves, become better able to concentrate and to deal with their emotions, and learn to cope better with childhood's many anxieties—for example, over school work, self-image, and friendships.

Early days
Children will already, in their play, spend a great deal of time in the moment. A toddler who picks up something she hasn't seen before and turns it, touching and looking intently, is engaged in mindfulness. However, much of what children do is triggered by adults, and their dutiful responses to commands such as "Brush your teeth" are likely to be automatic. A child, over breakfast, may be longing to get out and play or dreading that morning's arithmetic. Mind wandering, while functioning on autopilot, is very much a part of a child's mindset.

While adults actively choose to bring mindfulness into their lives through various types of formal meditation

SEEDS OF THOUGHT

An effective way to tell a child how their thoughts and emotions work is with this simple analogy. If a child is upset about something, this can also soothe them. You'll need a screw-top glass jar and a lot of small seeds that will sink in water—dry seeds tend to float, but many kinds will sink if you soak them first.

1 Fill the jar with water and sprinkle the seeds on top. Screw the lid on tight, shake up the jar and put it down in front of the child.

2 Ask the child to focus on their breathing while they watch the seeds, like their own thoughts, swirl around in the water, slowly sinking until they settle on the bottom.

3 Explain to the child that while they're thinking about their breathing, their feelings and thoughts are settling down, just like the seeds. They have the power to let them settle by simply focusing on something else.

practice, you may need some imagination and a sense of fun to engage children. A good way to start is to ask the child to choose a favorite object—perhaps a toy—and to draw it. Then ask them to look again, more closely, spending more time picking out more detail. When they draw the object again, extra details will usually be rendered. Ask how they felt about looking at something so closely: did they feel they saw the object more as a camera would?

Breath awareness also works well: kids will often be surprised—and amused—by how difficult it is to stay focused. Children may have difficulty understanding what it means to pay attention to their breath. If so, they can place a favorite stuffed toy on their bellies and focus attention on its movement up and down.

Exploring awareness

A natural progression from here is a variant of the body scan (see pages 120–25) in which the child attends to sensations. Ask the child to describe their movements around a room or yard. Tell them to move very slowly, since they're walking on fragile tiles and must try not to break any. Ask them to concentrate on what's going on in their body with every movement, and describe it to you. Telling them that they have superpowers of vision or hearing

> Kids will often be surprised—and amused—by how difficult it is to stay focused.

can make the exercise more fun, and encourages focus as they walk around their environment.

If your children aren't interested in one or several of these mindfulness activities, try another approach. Be mindful yourself, taking success and failure with equanimity.

CAT PERSON

This simple meditation (to be spoken aloud to the child) conveys an important message—that thoughts pass through our minds, and can be watched, as if by someone else.

1 Close your eyes. You're a cat on the floor, looking at the mouse hole in the baseboard, hoping mice will come out so you can catch them.

2 Every thought you have, apart from thinking about the cat and the hole, is one of those mice. Just sit there and pounce on every thought that pops out.

3 Are you so busy being the cat and looking at the hole that you don't think any thoughts? What happens if you keep doing it? A thought is sure to come along soon.

IN CRISIS
HOW TO DEAL WITH TOUGH TIMES

Nobody's life is without its share of problems, but in general we humans are resilient and adapt well to new situations. Mindfulness gives us another life strategy: by embracing distress, rather than fighting back, we give ourselves the best chance to ride its turbulence and keep our lives on track.

L eft to its own devices, the mind tends to run away from difficulties and toward desire. But some problems are so big and oppressive that we find ourselves unable to move beyond their shadow.

In the long term, we're being kind to ourselves when we choose to face our difficulties rather than try to avoid them. Putting a "spin" on feeling miserable is a way of fighting against the reality, and all inner fights are tiring and ultimately unsuccessful. The best way to escape a trap is to study how it works and then dismantle it part by part: you can't be trapped in a mechanism that's been taken apart.

Tactics for tough times
When you're having a tough time, your difficulties operate on two levels. First, there's the primary problem—which

MOVING BEYOND PAIN

An effective way to deal with pain, whether physical or emotional, is to stay in the present moment as much as possible, and from that viewpoint break it down into individual sensations, which change over time.

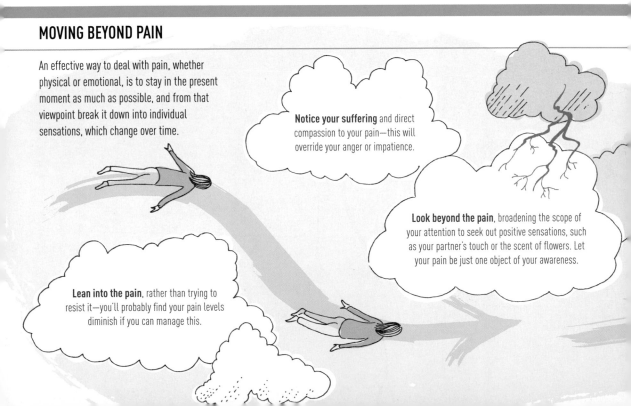

Notice your suffering and direct compassion to your pain—this will override your anger or impatience.

Look beyond the pain, broadening the scope of your attention to seek out positive sensations, such as your partner's touch or the scent of flowers. Let your pain be just one object of your awareness.

Lean into the pain, rather than trying to resist it—you'll probably find your pain levels diminish if you can manage this.

might be an illness, a loss, or a serious misfortune or disappointment. This is the reality you need to face, and make peace with, since it's factual and can't be reversed. The secondary problem is the mind's suffering. This is based entirely on our response to the primary problem; it often starts with a judgement—"this shouldn't be happening"—which in turn leads to an emotion, such as anger, fear, frustration, or hopelessness. The emotion can't be controlled or wished away, but its invitation to suffering can be resisted by an attitude of mindfulness. Some pain in life is inevitable, but suffering is a choice we make, based on our rejection of that pain and an acceptance of the distress it brings.

The truth of this can be seen when you mindfully explore physical pain. Try this next time you have a headache or backache or any other painful symptom. Attending to what you're feeling, you'll discover the simple sensation—pain itself—and, alongside that, your own resistance to that sensation. The resistance is partly physical—a group of muscles in tension around the pain source. If you can relax those muscles, one by one, you will feel the discomfort lessening.

Compassion for anguish

Just as you tense your muscles in response to pain, you might also tense your mind. It's possible to relax this tautness too, by a movement of the mind. This is the moment when you release your suffering. Instead of holding yourself apart from the pain,

you move toward it, with compassion and gentleness, experiencing it as pure sensation—letting go of the thought of how unhappy it's making you.

About knowing

Any distress in life can be approached in a similar way. This does not mean refusing yourself permission to have emotions, or letting your tears flow: it only means not giving distress permission to take up permanent residence in your being, stealing the keys to all your choices. Often the thing that threatens your well-being will be what you think rather than an actual sensation. It might be thinking about what has happened or what will happen. Staying within the present pushes thoughts like these into the background, where they lose their power to do harm.

Take practical steps to diminish the pain if possible—in other words, work on the problem as well as on the symptom.

Our ability to grow and change, and live as our true selves, moment by moment, even through times of distress, is invincible if we choose it to be so.

THE MINDFUL CARER
HOW TO SHOW PRACTICAL COMPASSION

"Be a rainbow in someone else's cloud," said the poet Maya Angelou. Being a carer for a loved one, though potentially stressful, can also be rewarding, refreshing your relationship with a new kind of closeness. The secret is to be highly attuned to both your needs and your dependent's—and to focus on the moment with them.

Providing someone with regular care can exact a high price on your physical and mental well-being. With time, compassion can become "compassion fatigue" where stress, anxiety, and negative attitudes dominate your conscious mind—feelings not helped by the low status given to caregivers by much of society. Along with this can come a sense of no longer being fully yourself, of isolation, and of low personal achievement—especially if you are helping someone struggle, with difficulty, through a chronic illness that has little hope of improvement.

The mindful approach is to sustain a sense of your own life while being responsive to the other's needs, to find

CAREGIVER'S CHARTER

Every carer's situation differs and we are not all equally equipped to deal with the demands placed on us. Respecting our own dignity, and the dignity of our dependent, is central to a healthy and positive relationship. These simple, mindful thoughts may help to guide you.

See your care as a flow of giving—in gratitude for what you've received from the person.

Allow gifts to flow back to you—for example, acts of kindness or thoughtful comments.

Give your dependent as big a say as possible—involve them in decision-making.

> Sustain a sense of
> your own life while
> being responsive to
> the other's needs.

---

value in present-moment experience, and to invest fully in the relationship, exploring aspects of the bond beyond the practicalities of care. Long-term carers need to ensure that their own empathic sadness doesn't feed back as negative energy. A positive attitude springs out of feeling positive. Being in the moment as much as possible helps by diminishing any regret for lost times or any anxiety for the future.

The thought, "This will be my life until I can't cope any more and I'm forced to seek professional help," is unhelpful because it's both speculative and reactive, but also because it's narrow in its implied view of your life's potential. Within the moment, happy times—of contact, laughter, and spontaneity—will often be possible if you can summon the strength to move out of suffering's shadow.

Bringing your own vitality to the situation can make that shadow fainter. In any case, giving is known to be an important part of happiness, stemming from a clear sense of purpose and from bringing your best qualities to the fore.

Awake to the other

Be careful to avoid role stereotypes—especially the idea of the carer as active and the dependent as passive. It's more mindful to relate to the whole person, and explore their concerns and interests, finding or continuing rich strands of connection. Don't let old disagreements surface. If tensions arise, be forgiving and apologetic—even if you feel no apology is needed.

Care of an elderly person can be physically taxing, and people in this situation need to attend to what their body is telling them about the strains it's under. Mindfulness body scans (see pages 120–25) are a good way of tuning in. Sharing your meditations can be a healing experience for both.

Anyone in the early stages of dementia may find that the emphasis on the present moment resonates well with their concerns about memory loss and their anxieties about the future.

MIXED WITH COMPASSION

Compassion can easily shade off into other emotions when you spend a long time as a carer. If you think this is happening, attend to your own emotions and note any negativity. Ask yourself if any of the following factors are in the mix. If so, forgive yourself for the feeling, but make a positive choice not to let it show.

- Frustration that being a carer was forced on you

- Thinking that you aren't receiving enough stimulus

- Sensing that the person doesn't appreciate you

- Missing your friends, and wishing you could go out more

- Not seeing a good end to your situation

- Looking back sorrowfully at happier times.

Socialize with the person—have friends around. Provide as much stimulus as possible. Spring plenty of pleasant surprises.

Work toward balance—find time to pursue your own interests and to see friends. Look after your own health through diet and exercise.

Communicate your love through touch and looking, as well as words. An affectionate look is highly nourishing.

Don't be thankful for quiet periods without tuning in to what lies behind the quiet—might it be withdrawal or even the onset of depression?

MINDFUL TOMORROWS
NOW LIVE THE FUTURE

Hopefully, you've learned enough by now to bring mindfulness practice into your life. Use this book as a reminder and inspiration, or go on to study more advanced texts. Above all, move deeper into yourself, connecting with the moment and living the story of your real-time experience, where true happiness lies.

Weaving mindfulness into your life may have changed you in a number of ways. If you felt stuck in a rut, unable to break through into fulfillment, perhaps you now feel that you're on a journey, finding happiness (at least in glimpses) as you travel mindfully, savoring your experiences.

If you previously sensed you were always falling short of your goals or discovering that once attained, they failed to deliver on their promise, then you may feel now that your hectic search has stopped. You're free at last to look around, rather than forward.

Don't worry if neither of the above scenarios quite describes where you are in your life. The mindful way is to focus on direct experience, which is different for each individual. During the day, moments unfold, one into the next, and mindfulness teaches that if we're present while that's happening, we have a better chance of not missing happiness through inattention.

If you've found meditation to be transformative, you'll wish to continue weaving this strand of experience through your life. By now, you'll know enough about it to be able to identify for yourself, intuitively, the best way to do so. You could, for example, read the sacred texts of Buddhism, such as the *Dhammapada* or the Heart Sutra, to stretch your mind. Or take up yoga, tai chi, or pilates to work mindfully on your body. Or just continue to draw nourishment from regular mindfulness meditations, learning as you go.

Many people enjoy the structure of an organized mindfulness retreat—these range in length from a day to week, and often include guidance from an experienced practitioner and teacher. Study the program carefully before signing up. Many retreats have a relaxing vacation component too.

Retune your practice

If, on the other hand, you haven't derived noticeable benefits from mindfulness practice, ask yourself why this might be. Could it be that your skepticism has held you back from making a full commitment? Have you merely dabbled, spending less time on the meditations than recommended, skipping them, or performing them only when you had a spare half-hour rather doing yourself the honor of making time for them? If so, why not try again, with more deeply realized intention? Tune into yourself, here and now, and allow yourself to live to the full.

The three gateways through which we connect with the world are body, speech, and mind. Follow mindfulness to experience sensation, connection, and openness, in the moment as it gives us its blessing.

YOUR HOME RETREAT

A retreat offers a rewarding way of deepening your personal practice of mindfulness meditation and learning more about yourself. If you'd rather not commit to an organized retreat, you can set aside a day or half-day to create a retreat based around your own home, spending an extended period in relaxed attentiveness. Keep the TV, computer, and phone switched off (make an exception for the phone if you're worried about emergencies) and try some of the meditative activities below.

Do a range of mindfulness practices—including at least two long sessions of meditation.

Take a walk, or do some gentle exercises or stretches— nothing strenuous.

Have simple, healthy, mindful meals, with no snacks and no alcohol.

Spend time reading and following other quiet pursuits, such as gardening.

Identify a small job that needs doing—such as cleaning out a drawer. Do it mindfully.

If you're creative, work for an hour or two on one of your projects.

INDEX

ACKNOWLEDGMENTS

I would like to express the tremendous gratitude that I have for all the teachers and sages throughout the years and ages, who have shared the deep and transformative wisdom of this practice for the benefit of all beings. And also to the many students in the mindfulness courses and workshops I teach. I am constantly humbled by the courage and intention they bring, the insights they share, and the resilience and spaciousness of their hearts. May all beings be free from suffering and may their hearts open to themselves and others.

Ken A. Verni

Very many thanks to Peggy Vance for suggesting that I write on this subject and inspiring me generally.

Mike Annesley

The publishers would like to thank Sarah Tomley for proofreading and Margaret McCormack for providing the index.